Memories of Bliss

God, Sex and Us

Jo Ind

scm press

© Jo Ind 2003

British Library Cataloguing in Publication data

A catalogue record for this book is available
from the British Library

0 334 02885 X

First published in 2003 by SCM Press
9-17 St Albans Place, London N1 0NX

www.scm-canterburypress.co.uk

SCM Press is a division of
SCM-Canterbury Press Ltd

Printed and bound in Great Britain by
Bookmarque, Croydon, Surrey

Memories of Bliss

To Ewan

For the yearning

To Percil

For the glow

Something which has existed from the beginning,
That we have heard,
And we have seen with our own eyes;
That we have watched
And touched with our hands:
The Word who is life –
This is our subject.

(1 John 1.1)

Contents

Acknowledgements

The people to whom I am most grateful are those I cannot name. I am, of course, indebted to the researchers, writers and academics who have gone before me and whom I do name both within the text and in the bibliography at the back. But while they have been invaluable in my thinking, of even more influence have been the friends, lovers and acquaintances who have personally shared their sexualities with me. Over the nine years it has taken me to write this book I have listened to literally hundreds of people, both through the formal setting of seminars and the everyday stuff of friendship, talking about their experiences of being turned on. It is from such ordinary things as chats about sex over dinner and giggling discussions with colleagues about school-day randyness that my understanding of sexuality has emerged. I cannot name all the people who have contributed to this partly because there are too many and partly because I treat such conversations as confidences. But to all of you who have shared in any way what being sexual is for you – you are truly the people without whom this book could never have been written. Thank you.

Someone once asked me if I had ever had writer's block. For me, writing is one long block, or rather it is the experience of getting blocked, identifying what the block is and then clearing it out of the way to be confronted with the next one. Varaghosa was very helpful at a time when there was a particularly formidable landslide in my path. On another occasion Nelson Gonzalez delivered two swift sentences that shifted an obstacle I had been battling with for months. I am also grateful to Varaghosa for teaching me Buddhism and to the Revd Dr Dennis Stamps and to the Revd Lizzie Hatchman who cast academic eyes over my bedroom theology.

The contribution of two communities – St Paul's church in Balsall Heath, Birmingham, and Worth Abbey in West Sussex, a Benedictine monastery – has been less easy to identify but every bit as important. Strangely enough, I have had some of my best thoughts while I have been half listening to sermons. I have no doubt that the half of my mind that was attending to the homily was informing the other half of my mind that was thinking about sex. But more importantly both communities, though very different, have offered me a living, breathing vision of God. There have been countless times when I have been among my people and gone home thinking, 'That's what I want to write about.'

I am also fortunate in having artists among my friends – poets, novelists, painters, sculptors, actors, architects, writers and musicians – with whom I have spent many an hour ruminating on the creative process and the perennial dilemma of how you balance the need to make money with the need to make. I am particularly grateful to Myra Connell, Jake and Gillian Lever, Helen McKiernan, Andy Broadbent and John Christophers, all of whom know what it is to wait and create. Perhaps their best gift is that of taking their creative work seriously. This is what encourages others to get on with their own.

Naturally, I have ended up talking about sex a lot. From time to time those with whom I lived in community for ten years dropped the hint that this was somewhat wearing. I am grateful to my friends for bearing with me. I also thank them for honouring my need for quietude, the periods when I had to ignore the telephone and would not go to the door. I appreciate Percil Cadogan for many things, not least being a guardian of my solitude. In the last six months of writing I was particularly appreciative of Bernard Davis, who inputted the bibliography, Alison Webster, who said 'Go girl', and Alex Wright formerly of SCM Press who understood this book precisely and championed its cause against the odds. Special thanks are also due to Arun Arora for thinking of the title, and to Gillian Lever for her brilliance and generosity in making such a sexy painting and giving it for use as the cover.

Finally, I would like to acknowledge my therapist, Shirley Wheeley, who died before I could thank her, and my mother, Ann Ind, who so much believed in my writing but who also died before it was published. I hope compassion and the capacity to embrace the darkest parts of ourselves are detectable within these pages. If they are, it's because I was first embraced by these wise, expansive women.

Preface

Sex is difficult; yes. But they are difficult things with which we have been charged; almost everything serious is difficult and everything is serious. If you only recognise this and manage out of yourself, out of your *own* nature and ways, out of your *own* experience and childhood and strength to achieve a relation to sex wholly your own (*not* influenced by convention and custom), than you need no longer be afraid of losing yourself and becoming unworthy of your best possession. (Rainer Maria Rilke, *Letters to a Young Poet*, p. 35)

This has been a difficult book to write.

It seems only sensible, in writing a book on sexuality, to familiarize myself with the thoughts, evidence and experiences of those who have written before me – in other words, do a bit of background reading. The problem with reading about sex is that the literature is totally overwhelming. There are some subjects on which you can read everything that's ever been written, the Nemipterid fishes of the world, for example. If I was to try to read everything that had ever been written about sex I would be dead before I got round to doing my own writing. As it is, I have read biographies, histories, anthropologies, sociological surveys, theologies, language theories, philosophies, poetry and user-guides to fetish style. I have read Herbert Marcuse's political preface (1966) in *Eros and Civilization*. I have read the sex advice in the *You* magazine of the *Mail on Sunday*. I have read the Bible. I have read *Fetish Times*. How do you decide where to end? In fact where do you begin?

My purpose in writing this book is to enable us to live our sexualities well. It is to help us to find our ways in a world where we are surrounded by a bewildering array of different attitudes towards sex. I am asking the question 'What is sexuality?' because I want to know how to behave between the sheets, out on the pull and over juiceless years when randiness is but a distant memory. My quest has been a practical rather than an academic one. My method has therefore been to use one criterion in assessing what to read and write: 'Is it useful?' I have endeavoured to find the words which will make a difference to the way we love, relate, pray and turn each other on.

Sexuality is conceptually tricky. There is no getting away from that. Thinking through sexuality makes rocket science seem like a game of marbles. In writing this book I have had to negotiate a tension between being understandable on the one hand and doing justice to the awe-inspiring complexity of the subject on the other. Writing on sexuality is all too often reduced to the banal. I once read a book that claimed to tell THE truth about sex – it included such insights as 'women don't like men with thinning hair'. It is partly as a reaction to such facile renditions of sexuality that I have felt the need to write my own account. I certainly have no wish to add to countless other trite theories. On the other hand, I don't want my writing to be difficult. My words are not going to be useful unless they are understandable. I have therefore endeavoured to tread a line between being clear, on the one hand, and doing justice to an impossibly complex subject on the other. To those who find my accounts of Freud, language theory and the Bible cursory and frustrating, I apologize. I also apologize to those who read this book with care who still think I'm making the subject far more complicated than it needs to be. There will be people on both sides of the line.

Likewise, I am never going to be able to keep everybody happy with the language I use to describe sex. I would be disappointed to lose readers because they are shocked by the words that I use. However, our collective discomfort around sexuality is such that it is very difficult to find words that are neither clinical, euphemistic nor crude. The nature of my argument means that I have to be precise, hence I use the clumsy phrase 'heterosexual vaginal intercourse' instead of 'sex', for example. Otherwise I have aimed to write about sex in the way in which people of my age speak about it in everyday life. I appreciate there will be some who will be alienated by my vocabulary, but by the same token a more formal language would have alienated others.

Another dilemma in writing this book has been working out how much to include my own sexuality within the pages. As the only purpose in reading and writing about sexuality, as far as I am concerned, is to bring us on in our capacity to relate to each other I have had to continually filter my reading and thinking through the mesh of my own sexual experience. If my words fail to touch my own erotic sensibilities why should they be of use to anybody else who reads them? In writing, therefore, I have had to be very aware of my own sexuality. I have had to heed it, listen to it, describe it, attend to it, laugh at it, be surprised by it and be prepared to use the delete button should I be tempted to put in anything that does not ring true with the way I moisten, desire and swell.

But writing which is rooted in personal experience is fraught with difficulties. It is easy to assume that because my thoughts have been filtered through my own libido, and because I am a woman, this must therefore be an account of 'women's sexuality', but I am not sure that this is the case. In fact I'm not even sure if there is such a thing. There is no doubt that this is a woman-centred book. Though I have read books on male sexuality and listened to male lovers and friends, I have made more reference to accounts of women's sexual fantasies and women's experience of intercourse. Whether this means that what I have written adds up to 'women's sexuality' is another matter. In rooting my writing in my own sexuality I will doubtless be reflecting some dimensions of sexuality that are particular to women, some that are rooted in my culture, some that are peculiar to me and some that are experienced universally.

Another problem with writing about sex from personal experience is that it runs the risk of being individualistic, and this book is no exception. The sexual ethic I espouse *is* individualistic in comparison to a traditional ethic which claims that the right place for sex is lifelong monogamous commitment and that this is true for all people throughout all ages. However, I believe the approach I advocate is one which has the potential to build community. It is one which enables a Caribbean Christian to explain to an English Christian why it is that in his culture there is a tendency for people to have babies when they are young and get married much later in life. It is one which enables a woman who is in love with another woman to reveal to a happily married man how she has come to relate more profoundly to a trinitarian God through her experience of being turned on. I hope I have written a book which is useful to people who, for whatever reason, perceive their sexualities as different from the majority. I believe I am offering tools which enable us to retain our integrities in a world where there is overwhelming pressure for us to do otherwise.

This book opens by asking the question, 'What is sexuality?' In the second chapter I offer a definition. This definition enables me, in the third, fourth and fifth chapters, to investigate the nature of sexual experience. Having established some insight into the way in which sexuality works, I go on to ask how we should treat each other in the light of the commandment that we love God, love our neighbour and love ourselves.

'Weave real connections, create real nodes, build real houses. Live a life you can endure,' says Marge Piercy in her poem 'The Seven of Pentacles' (Marilyn Sewell (ed.), *Cries of the Spirit*, pp. 171–2). 'Make love that is loving.' Writing this book has made me better able to make love that is loving. My hope is that it will enable others to do the same.

Jo Ind

Chapter One

What Is Sexuality?

I gasped as his hand landed firmly but gently on my naked back. Lying on my front chatting to Phil I had been anticipating its arrival but there was no mistaking my mid-sentence intake of breath as he touched me. I tried to remember what I had been talking about as his other hand greeted my torso and worked its way around my shoulders and down my spine in warm, stimulating movements.

It was not long before I gave up on conversation. Chatting had seemed easy when we were not in contact but it became more of an effort the more Phil's palms worked up and down, up and down. There was a sense of rhythm in his movement into which I wanted to relax.

On and on he worked broad strokes and small strokes, circles and lines, nearly round to my tummy, up to my hairline, my eyes were closed, my breathing slowed, and I allowed myself to be conscious of nothing at all except the ongoing dance of his hands. Slowly an image of a desert island came to mind: sand, sea and solitary palm tree. As Phil worked on my neck and shoulders I remembered sitting at my desk and I slowly dropped the stresses of the office into the water. What else would I like to float away? I thought of specific work commitments, of deadlines and seminars to come, of mistakes I had made, of opportunities I had missed. I let go of them one by one and watched them be taken up in the ocean.

Ironically I was actually working as I lay there and Phil was working as he touched me. Phil, short, stocky and good-looking, was the masseur for the Birmingham Royal Ballet. He worked on ballet dancers' limbs in Birmingham and toured with the company using his knowing touch when they were injured to quicken their return to the stage. I was a journalist for *The Birmingham Post* and had thought it would be interesting to interview him for an article in our weekly lifestyle magazine. It has to be understood that when I interview a chef I expect to taste his food, when I interview an author I expect to read her books, and when I interview a masseur I expect . . .

There was no doubt about it, this was different from the professional massages I had had in the past. My attention returned to his hands and I tried to think about how I was going to write this up for the paper. I had only had professional massages from women before. Phil's touch was stronger, more vigorous and thorough. It was also more musical, like a ballet dance on my back.

That was a good one. I decided to use that image in my article and I imagined that all my back was a stage and Phil's fingers were but ballerinas. It was the rhythm and different qualities of his touch that seemed like music to me. Gradually the ballet image was transformed into a symphony and I pictured Sir Simon Rattle conducting the City of Birmingham Symphony Orchestra. Phil's palms became the double basses, his fingertips were the flutes.

Sir Simon's face looked plaintive. Phil diminuendoed

to my spine and I remembered biology homework and naming the parts of a skeleton. I became conscious of my bones as his movements became sharp and small, working his way down each of my vertebrae. That was another difference between this massage and others. It was much more precise. Down and down his hands worked into the curve of my back, slowly down through my lower back, slower still towards my coccyx. My body ached with anticipation. Were they going to stop there?

They were.

Here I am, I thought, with a man I've known for only an hour and I'm wearing nothing but a pair of knickers and a few towels – one flick of those towels and I'd be almost starkers with a stranger. Has he been aware of that this past half-hour or has he been too busy working on what is to him just another one of those backs?

My guess was that he was, at some level, aware of my nakedness if only because of a curious confusion that had taken place at the start of the massage. We had met in a Birmingham hotel and done the interview in the lounge. He had asked if I still wanted the hands-on research we had previously agreed and he had taken me to a small room by the gym in which there were folded towels on the top of a table.

'I'll tell you what I'm going to do,' he had said. 'I'll do your back and work on your neck and shoulders because of that ache you were telling me about. Then we'll roll you over and give you a head massage. OK? So what we'll do is, I'll go out now for a few minutes, you get changed and lie on the table and put those towels over you. Then I'll come in and we'll get going.'

It sounded reasonable enough and in retrospect I can

see how important those words were. In effect we were
negotiating the boundaries. He was asking for permis-
sion to touch specific parts of my body. I was granting it.
If he strayed into other areas we would both know he
was out of bounds.

It was not until he had left the room that I realized
there was something I was unclear about: 'Get changed.'
I hadn't got anything to change into. What did he mean
by 'get changed'? Should I have brought a swimsuit with
me? Had I been embarrassingly foolish by turning up for
a massage without a change of clothes? What should I
wear for a massage? What could you wear for a back
massage? What had I worn in the past? I had stood there
not knowing what to do and had gone out to the loo to
play for time. I had considered the possibility that he had
meant 'get undressed' when he had said 'get changed'.
But why had he not said 'get undressed' if that was what
he had meant? Should I go and find him and say: 'Hey
Phil, you know you told me to get changed? Did you
mean that you wanted me to take all my clothes off?' I
cringed at the thought. How could I ask that without
blushing? Maybe that was the clue as to why Phil had not
said exactly that. He was a strapping young masseur. I
was an eager young journalist. Perhaps he found it difficult to stand in a small room with me and say what
amounted to, 'Get your kit off gal. I'll be with you
soonish.'

I had lain under the towels with just my knickers on
waiting for Phil to come back. Those had been vulnerable
moments. He had come in and whisked the towel away
from my back, quickly tucking the middle towel into the
top of my briefs. Trust and a few inches of delicately

poised towelling were all that protected me from almost total exposure. A voice in my head said he would be able to rape me. Another voice told me to trust and relax.

Gradually the fear of rape diminished as Phil repeatedly reached down to the very boundaries we had agreed and then massaged back within them. The more times his hands stuck to the rules, the more my fear was transformed into trust. And as the trust seeped into my muscles and bones I began to wonder what Phil would be like in bed.

I wondered if he had a girlfriend or a boyfriend. He had made no mention of either. I played with both ideas and then imagined him and a duvet and a woman with long black hair, him underneath, her lying on top and Phil reaching round and caressing her back as musically as he was touching mine. I wondered if sex was a bit of a busman's holiday for him, but I thought better of asking. It wasn't the kind of question I liked to ask with no clothes on. I imagined how delicious it would be to come home to a massage like this each night. Or would it be awful? Would you always feel you had to reciprocate? That would be hard work.

My thoughts drifted back to the desert island and I found myself dropping more and more things into the ocean. I remembered some sadnesses from past relationships, and I let them go. I thought of some regrets from my childhood and allowed them to fall away. Fear of death, anxiety about the future, I waved goodbye to them all as the great sea carried them on. It was as though the lotion on my skin contained the words by St Julian of Norwich, 'All shall be well, and all shall be well and all manner of things shall be well,' and Phil was rubbing that knowledge deeper and deeper into the fibres of my being. My eyes were moist. My vagina was too.

He returned the towel to my back, skilfully rolled me over without revealing my breasts and started working on the tiny, nameless muscles of my skull. It's just as well I'm not a man, I thought, because I'd be having an erection. Penis envy is one thing but right now I'm glad of the secrets of being a woman. As his hands worked around my head, the skin on my skull prickled and a tingling spread down my spine and across my whole body. When he touched behind my ears I could feel it in my toes. I felt connected in a way I had not done before the massage had begun.

'Thank you, that was really lovely,' I said as he gently laid my head down. The massage was complete. Phil left the room, I 'got changed' and he returned and sat on the table with his legs apart. I was being a journalist again, standing up, holding a brief case and discussing when he was available to have his photograph taken.

But I felt warm towards him. In a way I felt cared for. It could be said that Phil was only doing his job, but he had done it well and though he did not know what memories he had stirred or what fantasies he had awakened, he knew something about my body and he could feel that it had changed in his hands. Perhaps the most pleasing feeling was of a faith being well placed. I had risked being vulnerable with him and it was a trust he had not abused.

We made an arrangement about photographs and said goodbye, giving each other a quick kiss on the lips. I walked out taller than I had walked in, literally. I guess my cheeks were glowing and my eyes were sparkling. I was definitely smiling. Heads turned in the street as I strode on feeling relaxed, animated and sensual. I felt randy for the whole of Birmingham.

'But it wasn't sexual, was it?'

That was the question a friend asked when I came home and bragged about what I had been doing at work that day. 'It wasn't sexual,' he said. 'It was different from foreplay. It was different from sex . . . wasn't it?'

Well was it? I can't say I was so sure. How would I describe that experience with Phil? I am certain we did not have intercourse. I know the only parts of my body that he touched were my back and my head. I am sure I did not have an orgasm, but I know my vagina juiced. But which of these are the defining characteristics of a sexual experience? Is it to do with the parts of the body that get touched? Is it to do with the acts that are performed? Is it to do with the imagination, the images and fantasies evoked? If we are going to say that the massage was sexual, then was it not the very lack of 'sexual' contact (touching my breasts, bottom or genitals) that made it a 'sexual' one? Was it sensual but not sexual or sexual but not genital? What is sexuality anyway?

Is it sexual when I find myself wanting to look at the bodies of other women getting changed at the swimming pool? Is it sexual when a parent smacks a child's bottom? Is it sexual when I hug a friend and close my eyes to smell her, feel her soft cheek against my cheek and her coarse dyed hair? Is it sexual when I read something that is so true my whole body responds 'YES'? Is it sexual when footballers leap on each other after goals? Is it sexual when a woman is stimulated by her baby at her breast? Is it sexual when a man orders another man to lick his boots?

What is sexuality? Any ideas?

Well, here are five different ways of thinking about sexuality:

Some people say that sex is biology. It's a basic biological urge. It's an instinct that is hormonally driven. Sex is physical. It's located in the different brains, different hormones and different sex organs of men and women. Society – that's to say the laws that we make, the education we receive, the family unit we construct – is developed to curb and to civilize our instinct to reproduce. Sexuality is the natural urge of testosterone which is controlled by such socially contrived utterances as 'for richer, for poorer . . . till death us do part . . .'.

The notion that sex is biology is a very popular way of understanding sexuality, probably because it is easy to grasp and simple to communicate. People whose ideas fall loosely into this category include Desmond Morris, who wrote the best-selling *The Naked Ape*; Richard Dawkins, *The Selfish Gene* scientist who claimed the reason humans exist is so genes can be replicated; and Peter Stringfellow the nightclub owner, who says he has had intercourse with more than 300 women. 'What you've got to understand', he explained to me, 'is that it's natural . . .'

This way of thinking is characterized by socio-biology, a discipline that started in universities in around the mid-1970s. Socio-biology claims most human behaviour is rooted in biology, specifically in our genes. It draws broadly on Darwin's theory of evolution which contends that all species, including humans, evolve strategies to ensure that they reproduce. Human behaviour, particularly sexual behaviour, has evolved to ensure that the human race survives.

This concept of sexuality is often used to explain behaviour like Stringfellow's. In the early 1980s it was suggested that men and women have developed different reproductive strategies. Men maximize their chances of reproduction if they spread their seed as widely as possible. Women have to carry the babies so they have more investment in finding a sperm-spreader who will stay around and provide for them. That's why, so the theory goes, men want sex and women want commitment.

Popular though they may be, socio-biologists are not the only authorities on the sex scene. One of the most significant and influential figures is Sigmund Freud, an Austrian medical doctor who died in 1939. He specialized in neurological diseases and became particularly interested in psychological disorders through working with his patients.

Freud was the first thinker to develop seriously an understanding of the unconscious. He believed that everyone, including babies, has an unconscious reservoir of instinct, which he called the libido. When the baby sucks at her mother's breast the baby's libido is both satisfied and formed. When the breast is withdrawn the baby has no object for her libido and so she puts things in her mouth as a substitute for the nipple. Freud calls this the oral stage. Defecating is another significant feature of a baby's life. He calls it the anal stage when infants go through a phase in which toileting is particularly fascinating. Later this develops into the phallic stage, where the infant's pleasure is focused on her genitals. Freud claims that a child who develops properly through these three stages and others is in a position to form a mature genital sexual relationship. Neuroses are caused through being blocked in this development. Psychoanalysis is Freud's form of treating patients who have got stuck at any stage.

The ideas of Freud differ from the socio-biologists. Socio-biologists claim that there just is an evolutionary urge for men and women to have intercourse with each other. Freud explains how that desire comes about. He says the desire, while rooted in the body, in the unconscious, is created and developed through our earliest experiences. His theories explain how crying for our mother's breast develops into fancying someone, why it is that we enjoy kissing, sucking nipples and nibbling toes. In Freud there is not that simple opposition between the body's urges and society which controls them. He offers a way of explaining how society, in the form of the family and the infant's environment, take part in creating sexual desire. The sex drive lies 'on the frontier between the mental and the physical', where mind and body meet (*On Sexuality*, p. 83).

Following on from Freud was Carl Jung, a Swiss psychiatrist who died in 1961 and who collaborated with Freud for five years but then fell out with him intellectually. Jung is not generally in vogue at the moment, but he is still interesting to some religious people because his ideas can enrich an understanding of ritual and wholeness. Anyone who stands by that popular maxim, 'there's male and female in everyone', might find something in Jung to enjoy.

Jung thought Freud made too much of sex. He built on Freud's understanding of the unconscious but he thought it was organized in a different way. He believed that the psyche, or mind, is made up of three components: consciousness, the personal unconscious and the collective unconscious. The conscious part of our psyche is the thoughts, feelings and desires that we know about. But, he claimed, we each have a personal unconscious too, which is a pool of information that has slipped into our mind subliminally. It is possible to become conscious of what is in our unconscious. Dreams, for example, are a way in which our unconscious speaks to us, not in the form of rational thoughts, but through symbols and stories.

Jung was therefore interested in symbols and stories and studied mythology, including Christian mythology. He discovered there were motifs in myths that were the same across the world. There were themes that were similar in societies that were at opposite sides of the globe and that had had no connection with each other. He explained this by devising a concept of the collective unconscious, an ancient level of the psyche, inherited from the animals from whom we evolved and which is common to all humanity. Contained in the collective unconscious are archetypes, which are the images or motifs shared through the mythology of every culture.

Now, according to Jung, within every man's psyche there is an archetype that symbolizes the feminine, his opposite. It is called the anima. Within each woman's psyche there is an archetype that symbolizes the masculine, her opposite. It is called the animus. So when a man and a woman fall in love something very deep is happening. She recognizes, through the man, her own animus. He recognizes, through the woman, his own anima. The result is intense energy and infatuation as she discovers her opposite within her psyche and he discovers his opposite within his psyche. Sexual intercourse is a physical symbol of this union of opposites within the mind.

We have moved a long way from the sperm-spreading of the socio-biologists but another thinker on sexuality – the Pope – to a large extent takes us back. The Roman Catholic Church's official teaching on sex shares something with Stringfellow's understanding in that it is based on an idea of what's natural.

In *Humanae Vitae*, Pope Paul VI explains that the church's teaching is 'founded on the natural law, illuminated and enriched by divine revelation' (para. 4). The basic foundation of the church's teaching is the idea that the way we make babies is by a man ejaculating in a woman's vagina. This is said to be natural. This is said to be sex. Any sex which is not 'open to the transmission of life' (the papal way of describing making babies) is therefore not what God wants because it contravenes natural law (para.11).

The thirteenth-century theologian St Thomas Aquinas explains this:

> Semen is needed to be emitted for the purpose of generation, to which coitus is ordered. From which it is obvious that every emission of semen in such a way that generation cannot follow is against the good of man. And if this is done on purpose, it must be a sin . . . But if generation cannot follow an emission of seed per accidens, it is not therefore against nature nor a sin – as when the woman happens to be sterile. (*Contra Gentiles*, 3.122)

So contraception is a sin but infertility is not. Male masturbation is a sin, but wet dreams, presumably, are not. Male homosexual orgasm is a sin but lesbians . . . well, what are they?

The Roman Catholic Church says that sex is more than 'natural' just as man is more than biology. It claims man has a supernatural, as well as a natural, calling. The love between a husband and wife is more than unconscious natural forces. The greater truth is that it comes from God, who is love. Pope John Paul II says:

> Sexuality, by means of which man and woman give themselves to one another through the acts which are proper and exclusive to spouses, is by no means something purely biological, but concerns the innermost being of the human person as such. It is realized in a truly human way only if it is an integral part of the love by which a man and woman commit themselves totally to one another until death. (*Familiaris Consortio*, para. 11)

Finally, The Church of England comes to a similar conclusion as Pope John Paul II on the subject of sex. In *Issues in Human Sexuality,* the bishops conclude:

> There is, therefore, in Scripture an evolving convergence on the ideal of lifelong, monogamous, heterosexual union as the setting intended by God for the proper development of men and women as sexual beings. Sexual activity of any kind outside marriage comes to be seen as sinful, and homosexual practice as especially dishonourable. (p. 18)

The conclusion is similar to the Pope's, but the reasoning

is different. The Anglican bishops do not appeal to natural law. They turn, instead, to the Bible. This in itself is a very different way of understanding sexuality from any of the ones outlined above. It is different in that it is a historical approach.

The Bible spans an enormous period of time. One of the writers of the book of Genesis is believed to have been a prophet living in Judah about one thousand years before Christ, but the stories he was putting into writing are much older. The Psalms are believed to have been written over a period of 200 years. The Gospels were written soon after the life and death of Christ, though it was several centuries before the early Church agreed on what should constitute the New Testament.

Not surprisingly, over the course of more than a millennium, people's ideas changed, which is why the bishops use this word 'evolving'. The assumption is that the way we understand sexuality grows and develops over time. The bishops explain that in the days of early Israel, rich men had lots of wives as a sign of wealth and status. Men could have sex with all their wives and any of the slave girls that they owned and fancied. If, however, a woman had sex with anyone other than her husband she could be punished by death.

The Old Testament is full of laws and rituals which had a meaning in their time but which have changed for us today. In Genesis it reveals that when a man made a solemn oath he did it by putting one hand on the genitals of the man to whom the oath was made. In Deuteronomy we learn that a man with damaged testicles has to be expelled from the worshipping community. In Leviticus it says:

The man who lies with a woman during her monthly periods and uncovers her nakedness: he has laid bare the source of her blood, and she has uncovered the source of her blood: both of them must be outlawed from their people. (Leviticus 20.18)

If we take a historical approach to sexuality, we can ask interesting questions about why our understanding has moved on. Why was there a taboo around menstrual blood? Why did it change? Is there still a legacy of this taboo around today? Why did Israel evolve from a polygamous society into a monogamous one? How did the Israelites' belief that they were a chosen race affect the way they had intercourse?

Sexuality, when looked at from this perspective, is not just an urge. It is something that derives its meaning and significance from other factors, like the history of a people, their identity, the economy, even technology – think of the contraceptive pill. It is a view that recognizes sexuality has a history just as much as the kings and queens of England.

So there we have, purveyed before us like cheeses at a delicatessen, a variety of different ideas in response to the question, 'What is sexuality?' It is by no means an exhaustive list. In fact all the authors quoted are European and male. The ancient Indian Tantric tradition claims that human sexual libido is in some sense identical with the creative and beneficial energy-essence of the universe. Andrea Dworkin, the US feminist, says that sex is eroticized oppression: 'In a world of male power – penile power – fucking is the essential sexual experience of power and potency and possession' (*Intercourse*, p. 93). There are many more sexual 'authorities' who could have been called upon to display their wares, but my question is this: 'Which of them is right?'

Is sexuality the means by which genes replicate themselves (Dawkins)? Is it the potential in the unconscious that is formed through infant experiences (Freud)? Is it the energy to reconcile the opposites within the psyche (Jung)? Is it to do with the wise plan of the creator to realize in humankind his design of love (Pope Paul VI)? Is it something that evolves, reaching its peak in the ideal of lifelong, monogamous, heterosexual union (Church of England bishops)? Is it one/two/three/all/none of the above?

My head is beginning to hurt. All I wanted was a definition of sexuality. I didn't ask for all this.

The problem is that there is no single definition to be given. We have no consensus. There is no agreement on what sexuality is or who the sexperts are. Sexuality is not a thing like a VW Golf, where you can consult an authorized VW garage if you want to know how it works. Sexuality enjoys no such authorization. It is much more up for grabs than that. There is no single body of authority on sexuality but a range of different 'authorities' with different starting points, different methods of finding out and different conclusions. There is no higher authority to which you can appeal to sort out the overlapping and sometimes conflicting ideas of the sexperts. This is rather disconcerting for those who like easy answers, though somewhat pleasing to those of a more anarchic disposition. Either way, it raises another question, namely, how do we decide between these conflicting ideas? Why believe Richard Dawkins rather than the Pope? What is sexuality – and how can we know?

Say for a moment you take the related question, 'What is sex?' and put it to two different sexperts. What would they say?

Shere Hite and Kaye Wellings are two sex researchers who give very different answers to that question. Wellings and her team questioned 20,000 Britons to create the 1994 report *Sexual Behaviour in Britain*. In her questionnaire sex was defined as 'vaginal intercourse, oral sex or anal sex' (p. 137). Hite, on the other hand, became famous for her US research on 3,500 women which became *The Hite Report on Female Sexuality*. Her definition of sex is much wider than that of Wellings. 'Sex is intimate physical contact for pleasure, to share pleasure with another person, or just alone. You can have sex to orgasm, or not to orgasm, genital sex, or just physical intimacy – whatever seems right for you' (p. 528).

One is very specific about what sex is – it has to involve something going up an orifice. The other is so general it could include having a tingly feeling when riding an exercise bike. On the face of it these definitions clash, so which one is right? That is a hard one to answer, but you can make it easier by asking some more questions, like: 'Why are they using those definitions? What are their surveys for? Where are they coming from?'

Well, Hite is a feminist who wanted to find out about female sexuality and who discovered through her research that 70 per cent of women do not have orgasms through intercourse. Why then, she asked, is 'full sex' or 'proper sex' or just plain 'sex' defined in many people's minds as the penis entering the vagina?

Our whole society's definition of sex is sexist – sex for

the overwhelming majority of people consists of foreplay, eventually followed by vaginal penetration and
then by intercourse, ending eventually in male orgasm.
This is a sexist definition of sex, oriented around male
orgasm and the needs of reproduction. This definition
is cultural, not biological (Hite, *Women as Revolutionary Agents of Change*, p. 3).

Hite says we should redefine sex in terms of what gives
women pleasure, hence 'whatever seems right for you'.

Wellings, on the other hand, would never have been
able to work with that definition. Her research was
funded specifically to provide information to help pro-
mote safer sex and minimize the risk of AIDS. Her work
would have been meaningless if she had included in her
definition low-risk activities like nipple tickling or ear
licking or bringing each other to orgasm through handi-
craft. The high-risk anal sex, on the other hand, was a
very important part of her definition. If the survey had
been funded to reduce unwanted pregnancies in the pre-
AIDS 1960s then anal sex might have been classed as
'other sexual activities' rather than 'sex'.

The point is that, though their definitions clash, neither
Hite nor Wellings is necessarily wrong. They are defining
sex in two different ways for two different reasons and
once their reasons are understood it takes the edge off
the 'Who's right?' question. The same is true of the other
sexperts. Dawkins, Freud, the bishops . . . they all have
reasons for thinking about sex in the way that they do.
Dawkins finds it satisfying to believe that a complex
world can be reduced to simple principles, so he is pleased
rather than irritated by what others might think is a

simplistic explanation of sex. Freud wanted to know why his patients were neurotic, so he had to search beyond the idea that all we really want to do is reproduce. The bishops were under pressure to produce a policy on homosexuality because of the increased public presence of gay clergy. All these sexperts have reached their different conclusions because they asked 'What is sexuality?' for different reasons and from different starting points.

Sexuality is not something which is discoverable independently of everything else we believe about science, experience, philosophy, babies, religion, sexism, authority, capitalism or whether our own parents had intercourse. There is no pure truth about sex to be discovered floating in the ether or the DNA. Instead there are different ideas that are formed by different methods and for different reasons. The best response to the question 'What is sexuality?' is not to search for the abstract answer that will never be found. It is to ask another set of questions: 'Who is asking? Why does he or she want to know? Where is he or she coming from?'

Who is asking the question?

Errr . . . I am.

Why do I want to know? Where am I coming from?

Chapter Two

Whatever Turns You On

I was in the library at university struggling with a long essay. It was a summer evening in my final year and the essay was being assessed to form one-ninth of my philosophy degree. The library, made from concrete, glass, fluorescent lights and muffled sounds, was evidently designed by someone who believed numbing the senses focuses the mind. I was sitting at a joyless desk, rereading books that I hoped would make more sense than they had done the first time. The question I was answering concerned Coleridge's *Biographia Literaria*. The examiners wanted to know whether it contained a coherent system of thought despite its different types of writing. Within the *Biographia* there is literary criticism, some philosophy, a few anecdotes, a bit of theology and a touch of very early psychology. My task was to ascertain whether it fitted together as a rational whole or whether it was simply a miscellaneous hotchpotch.

I was thinking about Coleridge and then I was thinking about the purple finger nails of the woman sitting opposite and then I was wondering whether the guy walking down the stairs had finished work for the day or was just going down to the snack bar, and then I was looking at the red hand moving down the face of the clock and then I was thinking about Coleridge again. When I had first read the *Biographia* I hadn't had a clue what it was about. I had read some commentaries and then I had read the *Biographia* again, and then I had reread the commentaries and then the *Biographia* a third time, and now I was rereading the rereading and wondering why Coleridge hadn't done this work for himself. Surely it was his job to create coherence in his work, not mine. But as I read I was building up little pockets of understanding. Each time I went round I understood the psychology a little bit more, and the literary criticism a little more and the philosophy a little more and so on. I was getting to grips with each individual section, but I still couldn't see what all the disparate bits had got to do with each other. I was beginning to despair that I ever would.

Suddenly, I had a thought, or more precisely one part of my mind made an imaginative leap, while another part was staring blankly at the ends of the book shelves. In that unexpected moment I glimpsed how the *Biographia* made sense as a whole. It was like turning up the ace of spades, or whatever card the success of a particular game of patience is depending upon, and as a result being able to deftly send all the carefully piled up cards to their top-of-the-table homes. My one imaginative leap enabled me to see how those disparate pieces were interconnected; what's more I was able to see that that imaginative leap was what Coleridge had been writing about and that was why he had not written the *Biographia* as a straight, logical system. He had created a work which teased out the imagination of the reader instead.

It was an intellectual discovery but I experienced that moment of it all coming together as a physical sensation. I looked around me. The library was the same sterile environment it had always been but I was hot all over. The thoughts were rushing, bringing a flush of adrenalin in their wake. I wanted to carry on thinking but I was experiencing such a burst of energy that I couldn't sit still. I left the library, jumped on my bike and pedalled around the city, writing the essay in my head as I went. The creative whirling of my mind was echoed in the onward, circling of my feet/pedals/wheels.

Bully for me, you might say, but what has all this got to do with sexuality?

Well, when I say I experienced that moment of it coming together as a physical sensation, I mean I experienced it all over my body, including my genitals. I was aware of my thoughts and I was also aware of my groin. There was an increased pressure in my vulva and it was juicing expectantly. I felt deliciously horny. Let me put it more precisely. I was physically moist. I was aware of the blood rushing to my genitals. I could feel the pulse of it throbbing and I was filled with desire. Exactly what I was desiring is harder to pinpoint. It was not a desire to masturbate, nor to have sex with any person in particular. It was more of an all-over kind of randyness, a feeling of wanting to sit astride the cosmos. It was the sense of the inter-connectedness of life that had excited me and I wanted that same life to spurt up through my vulva and out through my pores.

It was similar to other forms of sexual arousal in that it involved a moistening and a focus of sensation in my groin, but it was different in other ways. When I have been turned on from looking at *Playboy* it has been more obvious to know how to gratify my arousal – lie down, wank and that's an end of it. It is quick and relatively easy to turn on and off. Arousal by Coleridge was less easy to satisfy, an itch that my own hand could not reach. It was more all-encompassing, a feeling of profound well-being. 'Happy' is perhaps too simple a word, but happiness was a part of what I was experiencing. With *Playboy*-type stimulation it is quite possible to feel depressed, have an orgasm or six and then feel even more depressed than before. Being turned on by Coleridge was the opposite of depression. It was a feeling of exhilaration at many different levels.

That time in the library was possibly the first time I had became sexually aroused through something that was not another person, if that's an accurate way of describing a dead poet. I was turned on by a mind – or maybe by the interconnection between Coleridge's mind and mine – rather than the sight of buttocks or the touch of lips. I was surprised because nothing in our culture had prepared me for such a thing, but I have had several experiences of being aroused by things other than people since. I have become sexually aroused when listening to music at a concert, when I have been engrossed in contemplation in a monastery, when I have been singing with other musicians and riding the music as a surfer rides the sea. I remember getting turned on through reading *The Feminine in Jungian Psychology and in Christian Theology* by Ann Belford Ulanov.

Doubtless I am unusual in being sexually aroused through such non-bodily stimuli, but I am certain I am not unique. I know a conductor who said of a piece of music: 'It goes straight to the crotch.' I have a friend who has been aroused walking through a bluebell wood. The poet Audre Lorde, in her famous essay *Uses of the Erotic: The Erotic as Power*, says: 'And there is, for me, no difference between writing a good poem and moving into sunlight against the body of a woman I love' (Nelson and Longfellow, *Sexuality and the Sacred*, p. 78). A guy in *The Hite Report on Male Sexuality*, says: 'I get a semi-erection if I peel out in my car' (p. 332). I have even known women who have orgasmed through such things. One woman has told me she climaxed when she was receiving holy communion. Another recalled a time when she was being driven through the Alps by a friend on the border of France and Italy. They were playing opera in the car, the sun was bright and the snow was shining white. The music reached a climax just as they rounded a corner and saw a lake with two strata of mist. Between those layers she glimpsed the castellated tower of an ancient church. She had an orgasm.

I don't want to make out that these non-bodily-stimuli sexual experiences are any more or any less important than they are. They aren't experiences I try to have, remember nostalgically or recall to arousal. I'm not saying they happen a lot and I am certainly not making out that jazz, Coleridge and Ulanov are my only sources of sexual stimulation. I am not claiming that my prayer'n'-philosophy turn-ons are any better or any worse than arousals that come through well-honed biceps or a very specific pressure being exerted on my clitoris at the right time. In fact I'm not trying to make any judgement about them at all. I am simply noticing that they are there.

And I am wanting to invite them to the party. When I

ask the question, 'What is sexuality?' I want to take account of these kinds of phenomena. I don't want to ignore them or dismiss them as a minority experience, sublimated or just plain weird. I want a way of thinking about sexuality that includes these turn-ons even if it cannot fully explain them. So this is where I am coming from – the experience of being turned on through things other than people. It is not the only the place I am coming from, but it is these experiences that are the most challenging to conventional ways of thinking about sexuality and they are therefore the ones I most need to declare.

'What is sexuality?' That is the question I was asking in the previous chapter. I am going to define a sexual experience in terms of the changes that take place in the groin. A sexual experience is one that involves an increased blood flow to the vulva and the seeping of fluid through the vaginal walls. Alternatively, it is one which involves increased blood flow to the penis causing it to swell. This is what I mean by being turned on. This is what I mean by being sexually aroused. Sexuality, therefore, is to do with the capacity to be turned on. It is the means by or style in which this could or does happen.

Some people are turned on by intelligence and integrity. Some people are turned on by six-inch stilettos. Some are visually stimulated. Others are word sensitive. Some people are blonde-orientated. Others are bum-orientated. Some are aroused by people that they love. Others find knowing someone a hindrance to arousal. Some are sexually attracted to those that they envy. Others only fancy those they feel they can master. Some feel randy many times a day. Others experience it very, very rarely. Some people feel sexy when they are lying on their backs.

Others can't be aroused unless they are lying on their fronts. We are all different. No two sexualities are the same.

So when I use the word 'sexuality' this is what I am talking about – our capacity to be aroused, the means by or style in which this could or does happen. (And by the way, no one's sexuality is as one-dimensional as I have just made out either. I put it simply for the sake of clarity but sexuality is rarely organized around a single feature as I have suggested.) I like this definition because it is spacious. It leaves room for being turned on by Coleridge or music or writing a good poem, as well as the sight of a buttock, the character of a penis, stockings and suspenders or the licking of ear lobes. It is an inclusive definition and yet, at the same time, it is precise. It leaves no doubt as to what I am talking about.

But, for all that I like my definition, it is not without its difficulties. One weakness, it could be said, is that it is rooted more in women's physiology than in men's. Some men might argue it is important to include some notion of desire within a definition of sexuality. For many men there is not an automatic connection between desire and having an erection. Tony Hawks, in his book *Round Ireland with a Fridge*, writes: 'I woke with an erection. There was no call for this – I wasn't in the company of a beautiful woman, nor had my awakening interrupted an erotic dream, it was simply my body's chosen way of saluting the new day' (p. 80). A friend tells me he used to get an erection on the X66 bus from Birmingham to Leicester at the point at which it crossed the town boundary on the Narborough Road, a happening not accompanied by any feelings of randyness. Another guy says he gets an erection when his children jump up and down on his lap. He would argue strongly that this does not indicate he is being turned on by them. He would class it as a non-sexual erection, whereas by my definition a non-sexual erection is a contradiction in terms.

I accept this criticism. But my experience is different. As far as I know I only experience moistening and blood rushing to my vulva when I am feeling randy, however diffuse the desire. I have no equivalent of a morning erection, or none of which I am aware. What goes on in my vulva is intimately connected with my internal experience of desire and horniness so for me there is no need to distinguish the two. It is possible that in defining a sexual experience as one in which there is an increased flow of blood to the groin, I have chosen a definition that is more apposite to women's experience than to men's. If I have, then that's OK by me. For at least the past couple of millennia our understanding of sex has been rooted in men's physiology rather than women's. I am only too happy to correct the imbalance.

Another possible criticism of my definition of sexuality is that it is too genitally focused. Andrew Sullivan, in his book *Virtually Normal*, has a way of explaining his sexuality without reference to his groin:

I have always enjoyed the company of women, sustained many deep, strong friendships, had countless, endless conversations; but I have never longed for a woman in the way that I have longed for a man, never yearned for her physical embrace or her emotional solidarity. (p. 9)

He understands his sexuality in terms of his emotional longing rather than his capacity to have an erection. I would not argue with this. I agree that a sexual experience includes an awful lot more than our genitals. During sexual arousal the tactile sense is heightened all over the body. At its most intense, even touching finger tips can evoke an internal volcano. Sexual arousal involves our thoughts, feelings, fantasies and innermost yearnings as well as our groins. By defining a sexual experience as a genital one, I am not in any way saying that the groin is the only part of us being drawn upon in being turned on. I am simply saying that it is changes in the genitals which distinguish a sexual experience from any other kind.

In defining a sexual experience as whatever turns you on, I am laying aside an assumption that is common to almost all of the ways in which we think about sexuality today – that sex is to do with the attraction between men and women. The word 'sex' comes from the Latin *secare* meaning to divide. Traditionally 'sex' is defined as the distinction between male and female. 'Sexual' has meant having the characteristics of one sex or the other. 'Sexuality' has simply been the noun that goes with that. The difference between men and women and the attraction therein is therefore the common theme between the differing views of the sexperts of the previous chapter. Dawkins, with his definition about genes replicating themselves, is talking about the fertilization of ovum by sperm. At times Freud seems to be claiming that men and women making babies is the outcome of successful sexual development. Jung takes heterosexuality as his model when he conceptualizes sexual attraction as the reconciling of opposites within the psyche. The Pope won't tolerate anything other than sex for procreative purpose. The Church of England bishops claim lifelong, monogamous heterosexual union as their ideal. The sexperts are all starting with the observation that we are male and female and building up their understanding of sexuality accordingly. Even the notion of homosexuality is rooted in that understanding. The term came into use at the end of the nineteenth century and derives its meaning from the inversion of heterosexuality. It is every bit as dependent on the male/female distinction as heterosexuality is.

In the 1930s an entomologist called Alfred C. Kinsey began researching human sexuality. His previous work had been classifying and recording the varieties of wasps and insects, but then he turned his attention to people. He asked 11,000 people hundreds of questions about who they fancied and what they did about it. Kinsey found that about half the population had had at least some gay or lesbian experience. He concluded that some people are exclusively heterosexual and some exclusively homosexual but the biggest sexual category is those who fall somewhere in between:

Males do not represent two discrete populations, heterosexual and homosexual. The world is not divided into sheep and goats. Not all things are black nor are all things white. It is a fundamental of taxonomy that nature rarely deals with discrete categories. Only the human mind invents categories and tries to force facts into separated pigeon-holes. The living world is a continuum in each and every one of its aspects. The sooner we learn this concerning sexual behaviour the sooner we shall reach a sound understanding of the realities of sex. (*Sexual Behavior in the Human Male*, p. 470)

As a result of Kinsey's work it has become very popular to think of sexuality as a scale with homosexuality and heterosexuality at either pole. While there are still plenty of people who will punch you in the face if you so much as suggest they are a touch on the gay side, there are others who will happily refer to themselves as a Kinsey 4, or a Kinsey 6, conceptualizing their sexual orientation in terms of a place on a continuum.

Kinsey is to be applauded. He was writing at a time when heterosexuality was considered normal, natural and what God intended, and homosexuality was a sinful perversion. To conclude that almost half of us are a touch on the perverted side was outrageous to a good many people of his day. We are indeed indebted to him. However, I maintain that thinking about sexuality in terms of a heterosexual/homosexual scale is no longer helpful. It is time to move on from thinking about sex in ways that are rooted in the male/female distinction.

There are many, many ways of being sexual. In classing people solely in terms of a heterosexual/homosexual continuum there is no scope for exploring the other styles of arousal which are just as much features of sexual experience. Why place people on a heterosexual/homosexual scale rather than an SM/soft-and-fluffy scale or a visualsexual/auralsexual one? By thinking of people as either heterosexual, homosexual or somewhere in between there is no room for the type of arousal I described at the top of this chapter, where it is not another person who is the source of the turn-on. Even when it is people to whom we are attracted, it might not be their sex, as such, that is exciting us. The psychologist Sandra Bem says:

> Although some of the (very few) individuals to whom I have been attracted during my forty-eight years have been men and some have been women, what those individuals have in common has nothing to do with either their biological sex or mine – from which I con-clude, not that I am attracted to both sexes, but that my sexuality is organized around dimensions other than sex. (*The Lenses of Gender*, p. vii).

Personally, I cannot say, as she does, that my sexuality has got nothing to do with biological sex, but I would say that sex is only one ingredient in the kaleidoscope of elements that contribute to my experience of being turned on. Generally I prefer sex with men, but I would rather go to bed with a gorgeous, intelligent woman than an oik of a man any day. Like Bem, I find the terms homosexual or heterosexual miss the mark in characterizing my patterns of arousal.

What's more, even for those for whom biological sex is one of the significant themes of sexuality, the terms 'heterosexual' and 'homosexual' are so broad and over-lapping they require further explanation. Some men get turned on by women but find they cannot connect with them in the same way they can with men. Some women fall madly in love with other women, but still hanker after emotionless sex with men. Some men marry, love their wives and love their children yet feel the need to go out cruising and pick up guys. Some women try for decades to have satisfying sexual relationships with men, but give up because communication with women is so much easier. Some men feel horror at the thought of entering anuses – even the anuses of men with whom they are deeply in love. Some women are turned on as much by men as by women, but for political reasons choose to identify as lesbians. Some men get turned on by other men but are so frightened of that part of themselves they become aggressive in their pursuit of women as a result. Some people fall in love with someone of the same sex and then they fall in love with someone of the other sex and then they fall in love with someone of the same sex. You could call any of these styles of sexuality homosexual. You could call any of them heterosexual for that matter.

I am not saying that 'heterosexual' and 'homosexual' are useless words. On the contrary I think they are very important. They are important precisely because we live in a society that overwhelmingly privileges those who get turned on by people of the other sex. For as long as we live in a society that conceptualizes sexuality as being about the attraction of opposites; that recognizes, encourages and sanctifies mixed-sex partnerships to the detriment of same-sex partnerships; that defines sex as a penis entering a vagina; that deters people in same-sex partnerships from holding public office; that engenders a deep sense of shame in boys for the way they feel about men; that makes people feel that in some profound way they are fundamentally wrong – the terms 'gay', 'lesbian', 'dyke', 'bi' and 'queer' are very useful words indeed.

My starting point, however, is not one that privileges

heterosexuality. My starting point is whatever turns you on – even if that's Coleridge, even if it's a polar bear. In my book the terms 'heterosexual' and 'homosexual' have a place, but no more than terms like 'visualsexual', 'audiosexual', 'cerebralsexual' or 'tits'n'bumssexual'.

What is sexuality? When I am talking about sexuality I am talking about the glorious, wide-ranging, intriguing, predictable and surprising business of being aroused. I am talking about the way we are moved by breasts, by kindness, by red toenails peeping through open-toed sandals, by wind skimming across water, by kindred spirits, by kissing down between the breasts, down around the belly button, down, down towards the groin. I am talking about the way our bodies are changed through memories, fantasies, yearnings, sweet nothings, the biting of buttocks, the word understood, the semen smelt, the integrity cherished. When I am talking about sexuality I am talking about the multi-dimensional, richly textured, embarrassingly sublime, muscle-tighteningly delicious capacity to be turned on.

Chapter Three

Body and Mind

We have arrived at a definition of sexuality. It is a clear and precise one but as such it is not one that tells us very much about the nature of sexual experience. How do we get turned on? What actually happens? By what process does this rushing of blood to the groin occur? What is involved in our becoming aroused? We've got a definition of sexuality but what is its nature?

In the next three chapters I will be attempting to answer these questions by analysing different dimensions of being turned on. In this chapter I am looking at the physical aspect of sexuality. In the next chapter I will be addressing the role that childhood and the unconscious have in sexual arousal, and in the chapter after that I will be investigating the place of society and its meanings. Having developed a fuller understanding of what sexuality is, I shall use the rest of the book to suggest principles for thinking through how we should treat each other in dating, mating and out on the scene.

But first, the body . . .

In common speech the terms 'physically attractive' and 'sexually attractive' are almost synonymous. That isn't really a very accurate synonym to have created.

There are lots of things we find physically attractive without necessarily being turned on by them – tigers, babies, homemade bread, butterflies. Nonetheless, 'physically attractive' is generally understood to mean 'sexually attractive', which just goes to show that the body is central in the way people think about sex. It is therefore the place I shall begin.

Clearly there is a physical dimension to sexuality. Indeed I have defined a sexual experience, and therefore sexuality, in terms of changes to the groin. But, as I said in the previous chapter, the groin is by no means the only part of the body involved in a sexual experience. In fact being turned on is a stunningly intricate process involving the cardiovascular, muscular, nervous and hormonal systems, to name but a few. When a woman is turned on the muscles all over her body become tense. Her heart beats faster and more blood is pumped to her genitals. Oestrogen and testosterone are involved in bringing about the rushing of blood to the vagina walls and the seeping of fluid through its permeable tissue lining. At first, only a few droplets of moisture appear on the inner vaginal surface but as the number of moisture droplets increase, they begin to form small rivulets of fluid, 'like raindrops dripping down a windowpane' (Masters, Johnson and Kolodny, *Heterosexuality*, p. 54). While this is happening the vagina begins to expand in both width and depth. The colour of its walls changes from the ordinary purplish red hue to a darker purple. The uterus is tugged in an upward direction, away from the bladder, and in so doing pulls its lowest end – the cervix – along with it. Eventually the lips of the vagina begin to swell slightly. The clitoris enlarges, the breasts become bigger, the nipples become harder, and the whole body is sensitized.

(Something analogous happens in men.)

Generally when this is going on we are so engaged with whatever or whoever is turning us on we are not aware of moving cervixes and darkening vaginas. It's only when something goes wrong with our bodily processes that we appreciate the role they play in sexual arousal. If a man has high blood pressure, for example, it can be more difficult for him to have an erection. High blood pressure strains the arteries, making them hard and narrow, which prohibits them from expanding and delivering the increased blood necessary for the penis to swell. Likewise, it is quite common for women to find their vaginas become dry during the menopause due to the decline of oestrogen produced by the ovaries. Sometimes we can change sexuality – the capacity to be turned on – through simple physical remedies. Taking oestrogen can help a woman to moisten. The drug Viagra has proved to help increase blood flow to the groin. The anti-depressant clomipramine has been used to assist men who ejaculate sooner than they would like. Testosterone therapy can boost the libido of both sexes.

I have been interested in the role of the nervous system in sexuality since I developed multiple sclerosis. I have got a minute scar in my central nervous system which periodically blocks the messages travelling between my brain and the lower half of my body. When my lover caresses my thigh during an MS episode I don't experience a smooth erotic sensation. I feel as though I'm being pricked by myriad little needles. What once was sexy becomes frightening and uncomfortable.

MS aside, it is generally true that the more nerve endings there are in a part of the body, the more effective it is as an erogenous zone. It is nerve endings that make the body sensitive to touch. The mouth, for example, has far more than its share of nerve endings which is why tracing the contours of a lover's body with the tongue or lips is often more sensuous than doing it with the finger tips. Kissing, licking and sucking are highly erotic activities, partly for this reason. As we all know, the penis and the vulva are very sensitive parts of the body, where the gentlest of touches can evoke the most volcanic of sensations. It is less well appreciated that the anus and the rectum are also very well endowed. In fact the anal region shares many of the same nerve endings as the genitals themselves. As for the perineum, the area between the anus and vulva or penis – that is well worth exploring.

Sometimes sexual arousal is caused through a purely physical stimulus, almost like a reflex. It can happen, for example, that a man out jogging has an erection simply through the motion of his shorts rubbing against his penis. This occurs in much the same way as the knee jerk elicited when a doctor taps a patient's knee with a hammer. I have known something similar in the 1970s from wearing the jeans that were fashionable before Lycra was invented. In those days jeans were worn so tight we could only get them on by lying on our backs to flatten our stomachs and tugging the zip up using a bootlace for better grip. I wore mine so closely glued to my skin that the mere act of walking made me horny because they rubbed against my perineum. Some women have similar sensations from riding horses.

Turning each other on is, to some extent, about

learning each other's bodies, exploring the sensitive areas and finding out which kinds of movements cause our partners to moisten and swell. Sometimes we are so emotionally engaged that the mere memory of that person is enough to cause the juices to flow. At other times stimulation of the clitoris is required.

The clitoris is an organ in front of the pubic bone, enclosed by the outer lips of the vulva. Ordinarily it is covered by a hood, called the prepuce. The sliding of that hood back and forth over the tip of the clitoris is what gets many women going. It isn't the only way to have an orgasm, as we know from the woman who climaxed during communion in the previous chapter. Nonetheless, a bit of direct stimulation of the clitoris can be a very useful thing, just as most men benefit from an up and down movement at the tip of the penis.

In her *Report on Female Sexuality*, Shere Hite discovered that around 70 per cent of women find it difficult to have orgasms through vaginal intercourse. While not impossible, it is difficult because the movement of a penis in and out of the vagina does not, in itself, stimulate the clitoris. Some women manage to stimulate the clitoris while there is a penis inside them through the ingenious use of pubic bones. One respondent to Hite's questionnaire explained:

We lie side by side with legs entwined, so that one of his legs is between my two legs, which makes one of my legs between his legs, with the penis inserted, which causes my clitoris to be riding on his front muscles or pubic bone. Then wriggling around. (p. 278)

Another woman said she had had an orgasm during intercourse with one particular boyfriend but not with any others. This was, she said, because of the particularly neat way in which their pubic bones fitted together.

Rushing blood, tightening muscles, sliding hoods, compatible pubic bones – all of these are aspects of sexuality. We cannot account for sexuality without recognizing the physical reality of it. Turning each other on involves, among other things, paying attention to the logistics of the body: 'up a little', 'down a little', 'not so fast', 'that's right – just there – aaaaaaaaaaaaaah!'

But having said that, it all starts to get rather complicated. It would be lovely to divide my chapters up into the neat and discrete categories of 'the body', 'the unconscious', and 'society', and present three tidy accounts of how each of these different elements contributes to sexuality. I can't do that. I can't do that because the body, the unconscious and society are so utterly interrelated that it is impossible to talk about one without bringing in the others. I've done my best to present the purely bodily aspect of sexuality. I've even gone so far as to talk about reflexes, tight jeans and jogging shorts. You've got to give me credit for trying. Nonetheless, there are limits to the extent to which it is possible to account for sex in purely physical terms and I have just about reached those limits now.

The problem is that the body is a very complex thing. It is not a purely physical entity any more than sex is. Our bodies are never the same from one moment to the next. They are always in process. We affect our bodily processes through everything that we do. I do not have impetigo on my face today because of the antibiotics I took last week. I can play fluent scales on the piano because I practised many times as a teenager. I'm white, because my ancestors lived in northern climes. I need to go to the loo right now because I've just drunk three cups of tea in quick succession. When we are talking about the body, we are not talking about a solid mass of nerves, flesh and hormones. We are talking about a constantly changing physicality, an entity with a history, something that is what it is because of all the things that have ever happened to us and all the things that we have ever done. The lines on our faces tell the tale of our smiles.

So while it is true that there are physical limits in the way we get turned on, it is also true that we can affect those limits through habit and practice. A friend has told me that she finds it difficult to masturbate with her right hand. She only noticed this a couple of years ago when she injured her left hand and consequently found herself struggling to give herself an orgasm with her right. Eventually, after an awful lot of effort and several failed attempts, she managed the feeblest of climaxes. How strange is this? She is right-handed in all other respects so it is unlikely that her preference for masturbating with her left hand is to do with the wiring of her brain. My friend puts it down to habit. She has used the same masturbation technique for more than twenty years and claims she automatically uses her left hand in much the same way that she automatically puts her foot on the clutch when she reaches for the gear stick in the car.

The point about such 'automatic' reactions is that they have not always been so. They become automatic through practice. Practise anything for long enough and the brain–muscle co-ordination becomes so finely tuned it feels awkward doing it in any other way. We are familiar with this phenomenon as far as driving and holding a pen are concerned. There is an element of this in sexuality too.

Experience impacts on the body in other ways. My favourite theologian, a Brazilian called Rubem Alves, tells a story about a lecture he gave to students in Maine, USA. During the lecture Alves and one of his students each took a bite from the same apple. Alves went on to say that even though they had eaten the same fruit, they did not experience it in the same way. 'I love apples, too,' says Alves. 'But we can never eat the same fruit, even if the thing is the same. This very apple belongs to two different worlds' (*The Poet, the Warrior, the Prophet*, p. 44). Alves explains that when he was growing up in Brazil they did not have apples. He believed they were a magic fruit because he only knew about them through the story of Snow White. One day his father went on a trip and brought back an apple which filled Alves with so much awe he did not dare eat it. He sat and polished it instead. Even as an adult, whenever Alves eats an apple it evokes in him that sense of childhood magic. For the student from Maine the associations were different. Apples reminded him of autumn, the yellow and red hues, the chill of the breeze, the crunch of the leaves. 'Yes, I love apples,' said Alves to his student, 'but, as you see, yours and mine, although they are the same, contain different universes. They tell different stories' (p. 44).

All our sensory experiences are like this. Memory and sensuality are utterly intertwined. One smell, one touch, one taste are enough to evoke in us myriad associations, strange or sweet, disturbing or gladdening, of the week before last or our days in the womb. This is the stuff of everyday life. As I sit here and write it is the start of August. I have just put some potatoes in the oven. Why am I eating baked potatoes on a hot August day? Because I have been gardening. I have smelt my next-door neighbour's bonfire and noticed that even in August some of the leaves are beginning to turn. The scent of smoke and the sight of russet leaves remind me of the comfort of coming home on dark, dank October evenings to a house with lights aglow and an oven filled with fluffy, nourishing spuds. All I had to do was notice the turning leaves and there I was hungering for autumn's taste by association. Association has a very large role to play in our experience. We are constantly playing with it. The smell of lavender reminds me of my great aunt's garden. One glimpse of a Citroen 2 CV on a motorway and I am taken back to the heady idealism of my youth and community living:

> The body remembers, the bones remember, the joints remember, even the little finger remembers. Memory is lodged in pictures and feelings in the cells themselves. Like a sponge filled with water, anywhere the flesh is pressed, wrung, even touched lightly, a memory may flow out like a stream. (Estes, *Women Who Run with the Wolves*, p. 200)

Because memory is part of the body, it is also part of sexuality. Whenever we touch and smell and taste and see, we are calling upon pasts, reaching deep into histories. Once, during a time of love-making with a boyfriend, all was going juicily until I kissed his toes. He pulled his foot away and recoiled in horror. Later on he was able to explain that when he was a child an old man up the road had asked him into his garage and had started tickling him, taking his shoes and socks off and nibbling his toes. It had filled my friend with fear, foreboding and disgust. When I did a similar thing, however much he knew it was his girlfriend doing this and not the old man, he recoiled in the same disgust he had felt when he was little. His childhood experience was written into his flesh.

In the massage that I described in the first chapter, there were a whole range of images – ballet, music, skeletons, seascapes – conjured through the touch of Phil's hands. Those memories were a part of my arousal. It cannot be otherwise. Whatever we do, whether we wear Calvin Klein Y-fronts or silk French knickers, whether we shower and scent beforehand or go for it in a pheromoned sweat, whether we slap each other hard or gently caress, we are turning each other on through the power of association.

Habit is part of the body. Memory is part of the body. My final point is that thought is also a part of our bodily experiences. Rubem Alves has another story to tell. One day Alves' father-in-law was at a banquet in which he was given an utterly delicious meal. He enjoyed it so much, he asked for more. It was sumptuous. After the meal, when he was happy and full, he complimented the hostess on her breaded cauliflower. 'Oh! No!' she said. 'It is not breaded cauliflower. It is breaded brain.' Alves' father-in-law forgot all rules of propriety. The fact he was the banquet guest of honour did not deter him. He leapt off his chair, ran to the bathroom and vomited everything. Alves asks:

How can we account for what happened? The 'thing': was it not delicious? Had not the body tasted and approved it? What physical or chemical changes could have occurred after the word 'brain' was said? None. My father-in-law knew this in his head. And yet his body did not agree. What had been good to eat before the word, ceased to be after the word was heard. What strange entity is this that has the power to bring to nothing the hard realities of physics and chemistry? One single word triggered the digestive storm. It was not the taste, it was not the smell, it was not the touch, it was not the sight: one single word . . . What gives pleasure – and displeasure – are not things, but words, the words that dwell in them. (p. 49)

To put it more prosaically, it is impossible to separate our thoughts from our physical processes. In Alves' story, the thought 'cauliflower' was an integral component of his father-in-law's digestion. It was part of what caused the secretion of enzymes, breakdown of macromolecules and absorption of nutrients into the blood. Likewise the thought 'brain' was an integral component of his retching. It was part of what caused the relaxation of the pyloric sphincter, the closure of the glottis and subsequent contraction of abdominal muscles forcing the food back from where it had come. I agree with Alves: the fact that a word can do this is, indeed, a very mysterious thing. I share his sense of awe that something as metaphysical as a thought can change something as physical as blood – but it does.

And it does in sex too. In fact the role of thought is even more apparent in sexuality than it is in eating. I have noticed that there is sometimes a minute gap between a sensation occurring and my registering the sensation in the form of a thought: I'm having dinner with someone and then I notice his knee is touching mine. A split second later I realize it isn't touching mine by accident and it's with that thought rather than the earlier sensation that I feel aroused. This is the opposite of the reflex-style arousal I described earlier in which there was no thought involved. Here I am talking about the times when it is thoughts contained in sensations that bring about the changes to the groin.

One of the men in the *Hite Report on Male Sexuality* says this:

I like intercourse more psychologically than physically. I get a lot of physical pleasure from intercourse but I can also get that from masturbating. The physical feeling of moving my penis back and forth inside my lover is pleasurable, but probably not as intense as a good hand job or fellatio combined with hands. Psychologically, though there's so much to want – the anticipation of putting my penis inside my lover, knowing I'm going to be surrounded by her, warmed by the inside of her. Then when I first slowly enter her, I want the instant to last and last. I like to stop moving, just lie there, and think and feel, 'This is happening to me. This is neat. I feel so good.' (p. 322)

Thinking and physicality are not two separate things. On the contrary they are so interrelated that it is sometimes more often useful to think of a 'body-thought' than the separate terms 'body' and 'thought'.

A woman diagnosed with the AIDS virus explains how it affected her sexuality:

> For a long time after I was diagnosed I felt completely asexual. The implicit, and sometimes explicit, messages about people with HIV which I saw on the television, in newspapers and magazines, in AIDS leaflets, and on the lips of many health care professionals and *Sun* readers alike, told us that we were diseased, infectious, a threat to the 'general population' and as such had a duty not to have sex or reproduce. As for enjoying sex, well we had no right to enjoy something that was wrong. The only emotion we were rightfully entitled to experience was guilt. The result being that an old self-destructive streak reared its ugly head again, this time in the form of compulsive eating. As a consequence of this constant bingeing I put on weight, felt full of self-hate, unattractive and therefore sexually unavailable. (O'Sullivan and Thomson, *Positively Women*, p. 96)

This woman was affected sexually through her diagnosis, but not through the physical effects of the virus. It was the change in the way she thought about herself that affected her capacity to get turned on. Happily, she went on to change her way of thinking and in so doing changed her sexuality too.

How do we get turned on? What actually happens? What is the nature of sexuality?

We get turned on through the body. Hormones, nerve endings, juicing vulvas, rushing blood and tightening muscles are all essential components of sexual arousal.

But the body is more than spurting semen and sliding hoods. It is also a container of memory and a holder of dreams. It is changed and is changing through habit and practice. The body is the site of thought. It is the means through which we think and is itself changed through thinking. When I say we are turned on through the body, I mean we are turned on through memories, experiences, habits and words – words that are written in our flesh.

Chapter Four

Childhood and the Unconscious

This is a difficult chapter. I have several difficulties with it, the first of which is a logical one. It's tricky writing about the unconscious because the very act of writing is an act of consciousness. As soon as you put something that once was unconscious into words it isn't 'un' anymore. To write about the contents of the unconscious is therefore logically impossible. For the same reason it is very difficult to verify anything that is said about the unconscious. If someone asks me if I want to have sex with my father and murder my mother, then I can, in all honesty, say 'No'. If someone asks me if I want to do this unconsciously, all I can do is shrug my shoulders: 'Who can say? I certainly can't.' When I was writing about the pumping of blood and seeping of fluid in the last chapter I was writing about things that could be seen and measured. In writing about the unconscious aspect of sexuality I am writing about things that by their very nature are impossible to know of in a clear and lucid way. In the previous chapter I was stating facts. In this chapter I can't state anything that firmly. I can only say things like: 'I like this idea' or 'This makes sense to me because . . .'. The nature of the subject matter is such that all conclusions are tentative.

In approaching this tricky and slippery subject of the unconscious, I find it easier to start by thinking about something altogether more tangible – childhood – and work our way backwards. In the last chapter I said that memory plays a part in our sensual experiences and therefore in our sexuality. It does. In this chapter I am claiming that childhood memories play a more potent role than any others. Sex therapists and counsellors of many different disciplines agree that our adult sexualities are developed and formed through our childhood experiences. Were we to go on an archaeological dig of what turns us on as adults we would find layers of childhood beneath the surface.

The late Harvey Jackins, founder of a Seattle-based style of therapy known as re-evaluation counselling, has done some interesting work in this area. He says:

> I had a client whose wife insisted he had counselling because he could only become aroused and perform sexually with a pair of long, white lace gloves draped over the head of the bed. Conditioned by the culture, she felt that it was just too weird, though she might have felt a similar dependence on black lace panties was 'normal'. Once I had his confidence, it didn't take very long to get back to memories of the very, very tough time in his young life when his only friendly ally was the 'cookie lady' next door who wore long, white lace gloves for her afternoon tea. Of course there were many later incidents which glued sexual feelings on to the white glove memories by re-stimulation. (*A Rational Theory of Sexuality*, p. 19)

Another example he gives is this:

> I had a client who could only become aroused if he got
> into a tub of warm water with his trousers on. Sounds
> strange, doesn't it? Once he dared to tell me about it,
> it didn't take very long to get back to his discovery of
> masturbation while swimming in his jeans in a warm
> lake. And it didn't take a long time . . . to get back to
> earlier experiences of tremendous condemnation –
> 'You wet your pants!' The idiot 'logic' of it is obvious
> . . . it sits right there. (pp. 19–20)

While this evidence might seem too trite and easy on
its own, it does concur with what therapists from other
disciplines have discovered. Ray Wyre has been heavily
involved in counselling both abusers and the abused
through his work at the Gracewell Clinic for sex offenders in Birmingham. He has witnessed many times the
connection between sexuality and childhood experiences. He says:

> Women survivors of rape and incest have had their
> fantasy life abused. If this is not recognised, and it
> generally is not, it can be confusing to women. Women
> are told not to feel guilty, not to feel responsible, not
> to blame themselves, but in the privacy of their own
> homes they may find themselves masturbating and
> fantasising about their abuse. When a man abuses a
> woman or a child he is also abusing the whole sexual
> way that person operates or thinks. Because this hap-
> pens and it is not recognised, women feel guilty and
> think that they are responsible for what happens. This

is another thing which the man had done to them and which they may not even be aware of. A woman, now in her thirties, whom I was counselling had had a dog introduced when she was being sexually abused as a child and she is still fantasising about the dog. She can't share that with anybody. It's just too horrific for her to share it. (Itzin (ed.), *Pornography*, p. 245)

It is easiest to cite instances of abuse because that is what most of the literature is about, but I am talking about more than that. I believe it is inevitable that our sexualities are developed through our childhood experiences, abuse or not. In her book *Where their Feet Dance: English Women's Sexual Fantasies*, Rachel Silver interviews women about their sexual fantasies. One story she tells is of Jennifer, who is a happily married, well-adjusted 34-year-old. Jennifer says that she fantasizes about her father touching her. 'That's it really, nothing more than that,' she says. 'But it's always my father. And he's the one getting the pleasure out of it. I'm not getting any pleasure at all' (p. 139). Jennifer traces that fantasy back to a couple of images. One is of her father tickling her in bed when she was a child. The other is of a time when she was aged two or three and her brother had a swollen penis. He came rushing into the kitchen and her mum asked her dad to have a look at it. Jennifer's father picked up her brother, who was very small, and was touching his penis because it was all swollen and red.

Somehow that image stuck with me. It was almost as if he was enjoying touching it, and that image has stayed with me. And I see that image again, differently,

or my father enjoying touching me in the same way.
(pp. 139–40)

I want to pause here and acknowledge that this material
is very difficult to deal with. In fact I'm beginning to feel
a little bit queasy just writing this. When I was doing the
research I really was sick. So let's take a gag-break and
reflect on the second reason why this chapter is difficult
to write. It is difficult to write about the role of the
unconscious in sexuality because by its very nature it
takes us into places we would rather not stray. We don't
want to contemplate the ways in which bath-time with
mother or bed-time with father might have formed our
sexualities. There is a social taboo around this and a
physical taboo. We literally cannot stomach it.

A third reason why I find this a difficult chapter to
write is that it makes me feel very protective of my
own sexual story. It is interesting to note that so far in
writing about sexuality I have given away some things
about my own. I have alluded to being aroused through
Coleridge, music, massage and pictures of naked women.
I don't share these experiences lightly. Nonetheless, after
thought, I have decided that I am happy for them to be
out in the public domain. But am I prepared to reveal my
sexual fantasies and explain the childhood experiences
that I believe have contributed to them? No way. And I
mean absolutely no way. I feel enormously protective
towards that part of myself. I will reveal it only to those
I trust to treat it with the utmost care.

It is precisely because of the strength of my feelings,
both the nausea and the need for self-protection, that
I feel there must be something there. If there was no

connection between childhood and adult sexuality then thinking about it would be more likely to leave me cold than make me vomit. I want to run from the idea not because it's a load of rubbish, but because it's all getting a bit too sexy for comfort. The dog fantasy, the white lace gloves fantasy and the daddy playing with me fantasy are not my fantasies and it is unlikely that they are yours. Nonetheless, there is a quality about them that I recognize – the sense of something hidden, something from long ago that discharges its erotic feelings to this day. I can say of those childhood experiences/adult fantasies, 'Yes, I've got a few of those too.'

In the previous chapter I was noticing that there is a connection between memory and our sensual experiences. I believe there is a connection between memory and our sexual fantasies, too, but there is a different quality to the connection. My partner was wearing a musky aftershave the first time we made love. I don't fantasize about that scent but when I smell it again I get turned on by association. There is a clear and direct link between the sensory experience, the memory and my being turned on. The link between my memories and my fantasies is less linear. There is more of a dark, wandering, cavernous connection between them. Carole Queen, who gets turned on through being put over her lover's knee and spanked, describes this in an article in *Skin Two* magazine:

> As with every possible building block of sexuality, we all have our various preferences. Who knows entirely where they come from? Even when we can make plausibly causal connections between our kiddie Macs

and our grown-up latex wear, our pirate games and
our adult love of bondage, our youthful punishments
and our later ecstasies, there seems a non-linear quality
to them, as if the road we travelled to adulthood
wound through dreamy, subconscious territory and
left unpredictable elements to everything. (Issue 18)

I think she describes it very well. It's as though our childhood experiences are raw ingredients which get put into
the big pot of the unconscious and cooked until they
emerge as adult sexuality in a different but related
form.

'Unconscious' – that is the cue for Sigmund Freud to
come on stage. If we are talking about a hidden under-
world that in some way informs our capacity to be
turned on then we need to spend a bit of time with the
chap who made that subject his lifetime's study. Freud
claimed that from before we are born we have an unconscious reservoir of instinct, which he called the libido. In
the beginning, in fact before the beginning if you take
birth to be the start, the libido is the instinct to survive.
That survival instinct separates as we progress through
babyhood and childhood and develops into the desire
for sex as well as the urge to stay alive.

From the time of our birth, libido takes the form of an
urge to suck. When we suck at our mother's breast, or
'breast-substitute' as Freud would call a bottle, we are
literally sucking for our lives. Without drawing milk, we
die. Freud claims that when we suck and when we fall
asleep satisfied from the warm milk that comforts and
nourishes us, the bliss we experience becomes a part of
our being. We remember it, but not consciously. Rather,

the memory is repressed and stored in the unconscious. This is the start of division of libido.

Later, when we develop teeth and move on to solid food we no longer stay alive through sucking but through eating things like potato and sausages. Our libido motivates us to eat and when we do we are physically satisfied. But we also remember at an unconscious level the bliss that we experienced at the breast. We try to re-create it, without being aware that this is what we are doing. That trace of memory or mental image becomes a source of energy, the basis of the sexual instinct. We strive to experience that blissed-out-ness again and are motivated to find other things to suck like our fists and our toes. During this time, the oral phase, Freud says the sexual drive is auto-erotic, meaning that it is directed towards our own bodies rather than towards another person. Eventually, through other childhood experiences, we learn to direct the libido towards other people and that memory of blissful sucking is reactivated through mouth-to-mouth kissing.

In the last chapter I said that lips were well endowed with nerve endings and that was partly why they were such effective erogenous zones. This is true. However, according to Freud, there is a lot more to it than that. He says that the lips are predestined to be erogenous zones because of their role in satisfying the libido in our earliest hours. We like to suck and play with our lips because of our unconscious memory of sucking at the breast.

Freud claims that it is because of the separation of the libido that fantasy plays such a key role in sexuality. A need like hunger is satisfied through food. What we are desiring in hunger is something as tangible as a full belly.

But the desire for sex comes from a more hallucinatory source – the trace of a memory of bliss. It is governed not by a physical requirement as such, but by a memory. It is out of this image that fantasy develops. Sexual desire is therefore intricately related to fantasy and satisfied through experiences upon which we can hang our fantasies. Hunger, by contrast, is satisfied by food.

What are we to make of these theories? Well, as I said at the start, it is very difficult to know how to verify them one way or another. In fact one of the difficulties with Freud, and there are many, is assessing what kind of claims he is making and therefore how you go about proving whether he is right or wrong. Another difficulty is that he is not entirely consistent. He wrote a lot and developed his ideas over the course of his life with the result that what Freud actually said on any given issue is open to interpretation. He's a bit like the Bible in that way. People tend to use Freud selectively, quoting the bits they like and ignoring the rest, which is precisely what I've done in my very rough sketch of the origins of sexual desire.

But that said, and putting penis envy firmly to one side, I like Freud. You've got to hand it to him for imagination – that account of fantasy is ingenious. I like very much the notion that our sexuality is formed and developed over time rather than something that pops out of nowhere when we buy our first bra. The idea that our adult sexuality is rooted in our breast-feeding, our defecating, our early explorations of our genitals and relationship with adults makes a great deal of sense to me. I resonate with the notion that being turned on is revisiting the earliest, most primal part of ourselves. 'The finding of an object is in fact a re-finding of it,' says Freud (*On Sexuality*, p. 145). Having an orgasm is coming home.

One of the things that is difficult to ascertain in Freud's thinking is how much he is claiming that a man and a woman getting together to make babies is the goal of the libido. At times he seems to claim that it is. During adolescence, he says, we enter the Oedipal phase in which girls have an unconscious desire to have sex with their fathers and boys have an unconscious desire to have sex with their mothers. In healthy development this desire is repressed as mother and father show that they are having sex with each other and are therefore not available. Thwarted in their unconscious desires, sons and daughters are motivated to get out there and form sexual relationships of their own. 'The final outcome of sexual development lies in what is known as the normal sexual life of the adult, in which the pursuit of pleasure comes under the sway of the reproductive function,' says Freud (*On Sexuality*, p. 116).

At other times Freud seems to be severing the connection conventionally made between the libido and heterosexual vaginal intercourse. He says:

We have been in the habit of regarding the connection between the sexual instinct and the sexual object as more intimate than it in fact is. Experience of the cases that are considered abnormal has shown us that in them the sexual instinct and the sexual object are merely soldered together. (*On Sexuality*, p. 59)

Freud is saying it does not automatically happen that our

libidos develop into a desire for penises, if we are women, or vaginas, if we are men. Rather sexuality is formed through a long and complex process during which anything could happen. 'One of the tasks implicit in object-choice is that it should find its way to the opposite sex,' says Freud. 'This, as we know, is not accomplished without a certain amount of fumbling' (*On Sexuality*, p. 152). I like this. I like it because Freud seems to be putting the urge to reproduce in a place which fits with experience. It is impossible to ignore the fact that most of us do, at some point, use our sexualities to make babies. It is also impossible to ignore that a man's ejaculation has a reproductive function, even if a woman's orgasm does not. Clearly sexuality has got something to do with the continuation of the species, the question is what?

I like the idea that the libido, or life-force, is the urge to survive. I guess this could include the urge for the race, or genes, to survive as well as the urge for us to survive as individuals, though that is not what Freud said as such. What Freud said, and what we all know from experience, is that the things that turn us on are not necessarily the means through which we make babies. There are a wide range of things that arouse us – pinching nipples, sucking toes, slapping bottoms, licking vulvas, stroking cats, whipping slaves, wearing leather, making music, sharing fears and dreams. Our libidinous instinct has the potential to be 'soldered' onto anything. For some a man releasing sperm in a woman's vagina is the ultimate sexual pleasure. For others, in fact for most women if Hite's research is accurate, it isn't the ultimate turn-on but it is something from which they can derive a great deal of happiness. For others heterosexual vaginal intercourse isn't a pleasure at all. The instinct for survival does not automatically develop into being turned on through the release of sperm into the vulva. All of us are aroused through a much wider variety of stimuli than that. We must 'loosen the bond that exists in our thoughts between instinct and object', said Freud (*On Sexuality*, p. 59).

I also find Freud's notion of repression very useful. Some see repression as counter to sexuality, as though all we have to do to have a healthy sex life is rid ourselves of a supposed Victorian legacy of guilt. Freud, on the other hand, says it is repression that gives sex its currency. Our memory of bliss at the breast is repressed. Our desire to have sex with our parents is repressed. It is, he says, the repression of our contradictory drives and desires that forms the libido. I like this idea because it makes sense of the 'ugh' that I was expressing at the top of this chapter. In my experience there is a fine line between eroticism and disgust. The very thing that was so orgasmic in the bedroom seems ghastly while waiting for the kettle to boil – I wasn't doing *that*, was I? The more we reach out and live out our wildest fantasies, the closer we are to dancing on the edge of revulsion. The more we scrutinize where our sexual desires have come from the more we realize they are kept unconscious for good reason.

For all of these reasons I like Freud. As I said at the top of the chapter, I am by no means claiming certainty around his theories. They raise as many questions as they answer and sometimes they conflict. Personally I am more convinced by his analysis of the oral, anal and phallic stages than I am by his rendition of the Oedipus complex. Nonetheless I am certain that we cannot understand sexuality without accounting for the unconscious in some way. I am also convinced that our childhood experiences have a key role to play in the sexual adults we become. Whether the unconscious is organized exactly as Freud says, I would not know. But I do know that were we to dispense with Freud, we would need something pretty like him in his stead.

Chapter Five

Society and Meanings

We tend to experience our sexualities as intensely personal. Our capacity to be turned on feels as though it is innately 'ours' rather than something that is affected by such things as the Equal Pay Act, the invention of the jet engine or Sir Walter Raleigh's bringing back of tobacco from the Americas. We understand that our appreciation of music, manners, hemlines and hairstyles is formed and developed through culture. Sexuality, we feel, is different. It comes from the raw, animal parts of ourselves that could never be tamed through mere social forces.

This is a compelling way of thinking, one that resonates with those times when desire comes upon us in a pure, unbridled 'phroaar'. It is, however, mistaken. While it is true that our sexualities are rooted in the body and the unconscious, as I have described in the past two chapters, it is also true that they are formed and developed through the codes and conventions of the society of which we are a part. That is what this chapter is about.

The Tchhikrin Indians of the Amazon find it sexy to bite each other's eyelashes. Surma women in south-west Ethiopia make themselves attractive by inserting wooden plates into their lower lips. In Britain it is considered an insult to say a woman has got a big bum but in Africa and the Caribbean women with large, protruding bottoms are admired and experienced as sexy. In China, for the best part of a millennium, it was considered a turn-on for women to hobble around on broken feet just four inches long. Oral stimulation of the genitals is arousing in the West, but not in Nigeria or Japan. In some South Sea Island societies they go in for pulling, prodding and tickling the penis and vagina. When the Australian author Julian Robinson visited Kalimantan in Indonesia the local men laughed at him because he had no studs, rings or bars in his penis. They said he would never be able to satisfy a woman without them. This turned out to be true.

How does this happen? How can something as personal as sexuality be culturally constructed? How can my turn-ons be caused by anything other than me and the hands of my lover moving sensuously around my body? The relationship between sexuality and society is extremely complex. There isn't one simple answer to those questions. Rather our libidos are connected to the rest of the world through an intricate web of interwoven strands. There are so many of those strands I cannot possibly hope to chart them comprehensively. I can, however, pick out just a few of the connections.

In chapter three I explained that the body is not a fixed physical entity but is constantly in process, changed and changing through our habits and thoughts. If we also appreciate that our habits and thoughts are not entirely our own inventions but are influenced by our societies, we can see that our capacity to be aroused, as well as being instinctive, is also, to some extent, culturally constructed.

Let's take smoking as an example. There is a connection between smoking and sexuality. In the short term smoking can make us randy but in the long term it contributes to the hardening of arteries which is one of the leading causes of impotence. Even before they reach the age of 50, men who smoke are 50 per cent more likely to be impotent than non-smokers (*American Journal of Epidemiology*, 1994). And why do men smoke? Partly because they can. There was no smoking in Europe before the end of the fifteenth century simply because they didn't have tobacco. We also know that smoking is related to social class: the habit is twice as common among unskilled manual men in Britain as it is among professionals. And smoking is related to our beliefs about smoking. At the start of the twentieth century, it was believed tobacco had medicinal properties, with the result that just after the Second World War most men smoked – 82 per cent of them to be precise. By the year 2000, when it was understood that smoking can 'seriously damage your health', only 29 per cent of men smoked. (Smoking figures from ASH – *www.ash.org.uk*.) In other words a man's capacity to have an erection is affected by smoking and whether or not he smokes is related to social class, the availability of tobacco and the knowledge we share, as a society, about nicotine poisoning. Our sexualities seem to be very private parts of ourselves, and indeed they are, but even something as personal as a hard-on can be affected by public health policy and the long-term impact of Sir Walter Raleigh's voyage to the Americas.

In the last chapter we recognized that our childhood experiences play a role in the development of our adult sexualities. I quoted Carole Queen from *Skin Two* magazine who claims that there is a connection, albeit a dreamy, non-linear one, between her desire to be put over her partner's knee and spanked and the times this happened to her as a child. Now it happens that the way in which we punish children is a matter of considerable public debate. In Victorian times corporal punishment of children was routine and widespread. Since then it has come to be considered socially unacceptable. It was banned in all British state schools in 1986 and in private schools in 1998. At the time of writing, parents retain the right to spank their own children but how often and how hard and under what circumstances is something we, along with the European Court of Human Rights, are trying to ascertain. What is certain, however, is that ritualized spankings – 'come in, stand there, bend over' – are considerably less common than they used to be. If Carole Queen's story is anything to go by, this change affects not just our experience of being punished but our sexualities too.

There is also some suggestion that there is a connection between sexuality and public and economic status. In the late 1960s the US feminist Nancy Friday interviewed women about their sexual fantasies. She published the results in a book called *My Secret Garden* which came out in 1973. She did further research nearly twenty years later and published *Women on Top* in 1991. Friday discovered that over the course of nearly twenty years, women's sexual fantasies had changed. In the late 1960s and early 1970s women tended to cast themselves in passive roles in their sexual imaginations. They would fantasize about 'being taken' by an anonymous stranger. When Friday did her second wave of research in the late 1980s, she found that women imagined themselves in more active positions. In fact women were just as likely to fantasize about 'taking' men as 'being taken' by them. Now, it happens that the 1970s and 1980s were critical decades in the political and economic development of Western women. Friday's research was with US women, but landmarks of the British women's movement include the Equal Pay Act of 1970, the Sex Discrimination Act and Equal Opportunities Commission of 1975 and the first woman to become Prime Minister in 1979. Some of the women Friday interviewed in her second book had been born in the late 1960s. By the time they were developing their sexual fantasies women were in positions of power in a way unimaginable to the generations that preceded them. She says:

> Their voices sound like a new race of women compared to those in *My Secret Garden* . . . These women's voices make it undeniably clear that our erotic fantasies have changed in juxtaposition to what has happened in the past years. (pp. 4, 7)

So here we have three examples of ways in which our libidos, so seemingly personal, are not entirely our own after all. Our sexualities are affected by our bodily habits, which in turn are related to social class and medical knowledge. They are developed through our earliest experiences, which are influenced by social beliefs and conventions about the treatment of children. There is also some evidence that the ways in which we cast ourselves in the private world of our sexual fantasies are related to the roles in which we experience ourselves in the public world of politics and work. Nothing exists in isolation. Everything in the universe is connected to everything else and our sexualities are part of the universe. A butterfly flaps its wings in Beijing and causes a hurricane off the coast of Florida. An eighteenth-century explorer discovers rubber and causes a twenty-first-century woman to masturbate over an image of a shiny basque in *Fetish Times*.

In chapter three I said that associations have a considerable role to play in our sexual arousal. We've had plenty of examples of that so far – the woman who got aroused through imagining games with daddy, the man who depended upon white, lace gloves on the bed-head for his turn-ons. I once fell in love with a man whose hair was a distinctive shade of hoary grey. To this day if I glimpse that particular colour hair when I am walking down a street, it sends a message straight to my crotch. But not all our associations are so peculiar to our personal experience. There are many that we, as a society, share. Blonde hair on a woman has particular associations in British culture, namely of being dumb, fun and sexually available. A French accent is suggestive to many an English woman of fine food, romance and the most sensuous of seductions. In chapter three, I quoted a woman whose sexuality was affected through being diagnosed with the AIDS virus. She associated AIDS with being guilty, diseased, infectious and duty-bound not to have sex or reproduce. In this chapter the point I am making is that she did not think up those associations all on her own. She imbibed them from the rest of society

– AIDS leaflets, health care professionals and readers of the *Sun* alike.

We are beginning to glimpse another way in which sexuality and society are interwoven. They are connected through the associations that are made through our common way of life. Some of our erotic associations are peculiar to our personal experiences but many are drawn from the pool of imagery we share. In his book *The Quest for Human Beauty,* Julian Robinson shows the role that association plays in the sexualities of different societies down the ages and across the globe. Anthropologists, according to Robinson, claim that when tribes feel under threat from neighbouring clans, they tend to exaggerate the differences between them. This makes their own people more attractive to each other and less attractive to the enemy who might otherwise want to breed with them. The Surma women of south-west Ethiopia go to great lengths to distend their lower lips. First they put very small plates into the flesh. They wear those for some time and then gradually insert larger and larger ones until the lips have stretched to such an extent they can hold plates you could eat your dinner off. This practice, it is believed, originated from the days when they were in conflict with neighbours whose lips were less protuberant than theirs. In Surma society, therefore, small lips became undesirable through association with the encroaching enemy, while distended lips became erotic through the same process (pp. 76–7).

A similar explanation is given about the practice of foot binding in nineteenth-century China. Throughout most of the nineteenth century and some of the twentieth, it was the practice to crush the bones in the feet of two-

year-old girls and bind them to prevent them from growing more than four inches long. Nobody quite knows
how this custom originated, but it is generally believed it
was first practised on concubines of the emperor as a display of his wealth. Women who hobbled rather than
walked could not easily work and thus an array of concubines with bound feet showed the man who owned
them was rich enough to keep them all – the nineteenth-
century equivalent of a chap flashing his Rolex. Bound
feet therefore became sexy through their associations
with glamour and wealth. Some anthropologists believe
this practice spread most quickly in those regions of
China which bordered on Tartar territory. There is
evidence that the Tartars had feet that were naturally
bigger than those of the Chinese. The practice of binding
feet therefore took off on the Chinese side of the border
while the Tartar men developed a penchant for women
wearing long, curved shoes (pp. 75–6).

I think the neatest way of thinking about the role that
association plays in the way we perceive the body is to
think of the body, and the ways in which we use it, as a
kind of language. I am using the term 'language' in
a broad sense. It is a language in the same way that
music, art and Morse code are – they are all forms of
communication. Now, in any language, even verbal ones,
association has a very large role to play. Consciously, or
unconsciously, we use our bodily associations as a way
of expressing ourselves. When a woman decides to dye
her hair blonde, she is putting out a message. So is the
Surma woman inserting a lip plate. So is the guy who
gets a tattoo. In everything we do, whether that be
styling our hair, speaking sharply, wearing a miniskirt or

looking someone in the eye, we are 'saying' something. Whether we peck on one cheek or two, whether we sit on a crowded tube with knees together or legs wide apart, whether we shake someone's hand warmly or drop it like a limp fish, we are using the body as a means of communication. The body is not just the means through which we eat, sleep and stay alive. It is also the way in which we 'speak'.

The reason I believe it is useful to think of the body as a kind of language is that it enables us to appreciate the role that context plays in the ways in which we experience it. In any language, context and meaning are utterly interdependent. We cannot understand something unless we know where it is coming from. What does 'wicked' mean? Does it mean 'evil' or does it mean 'cool'? What does 'cool' mean? Does it mean 'fab' or the opposite of 'hot'? What does 'hot' mean? 'Thirty degrees centigrade' or 'sexy, fab and cool'? We don't know. We can't tell from the words alone. We have to read the meanings from the context.

It's the same with body language. What does a long, bushy beard mean? In the context of a certain style of Islamic dress we read it as a sign of religious zeal. On a pin-striped chap working in the City it would raise doubts about his professionalism. On a woman it would mean something different altogether. Though we aren't conscious of it, we 'read' the body in a very similar way to the way in which we read words on a page. If I was to leave my house in Birmingham and go to work wearing nothing from the waist up apart from some beaded necklaces dangling around my naked breasts, I would expect to cause a few erections along the way. I'd also expect to get arrested. But a Himba woman could go about her business on the northern border of Namibia wearing her native dress of a leather skirt, ankle bracelets and jewellery between her breasts without raising so much as an eyebrow, never mind a penis. The difference in those two situations is not the breasts. It's the context.

And what provides the context? Now you can see why I think this point is so important in a chapter concerning the connections between sexuality and society. Everything in the world around us has the potential to be the context through which we read the body. Politics, economics, medicine, technology, religion, law – all of these can contribute to our perception of well-toned pecs, naked breasts or buttocks peeping out through slits in jeans.

In Britain during the 1970s and 1980s it was quite common for people to be sun-tan orientated. Many Caucasians felt sexy when they were tanned and were more likely to fancy people with luscious brown limbs than those that were white and pasty. Getting a tan was part of the purpose of going on holiday. In Elizabethan days, by contrast, it was porcelain white skin that was considered erotic. Four or five hundred years ago people would artificially whiten their faces using lead, just as they darken their limbs using false tan today. In the sixteenth century white skin was associated with the court and the élite few who were rich enough to stay indoors, whereas tanned skin was associated with being a labourer and working out in the fields whatever the weather. White skin was sexy and aspirational, whereas brown skin was common and boring. By the end of the twentieth century those meanings had been almost totally inverted. Tanned skin no longer meant you were poor and worked outside. On the contrary, it was associated with being rich, or at least rich enough to laze around on beaches far away from the greyness of a damp English winter. So when a Caucasian Briton in the 1970s or 1980s went 'phroaar' at the sight of a bronzed torso, he or she was being turned on not just by a body, but by a body in context. The context of late twentieth-century Britain was one in which even the lowest paid tended to work indoors, in which it was believed having a tan was indicative of glowing, good health and in which holidays in the sun were the aspiration of the masses. Anything has the potential to be the context through which the body is read. Evidently the industrial revolution has had a bearing on the way in which we perceive the colour of skin. So has the availability of package holidays abroad, all of which lead us to a very strange conclusion – that our sexualities have been affected by the invention of the jet engine.

I said that the last chapter was difficult. This chapter is conceptually harder. Thinking through the relationship between sexuality and society is tricky, not least because it is unfamiliar to us. It is much more common just to think of sex as a biological urge and leave it at that. Casting the body, and the way in which we use it, as a kind of language involves taking on board ideas that for many are new and hard to grapple with. But it's worth the effort. In fact in my opinion it is essential to include a notion of the body as language within an understanding of sex. Without some reference to context and meaning it is impossible to explain why baring a breast in a strip club is different from baring a breast to feed a baby,

which is different from baring a breast for a mammo-
gram, which is different from baring a breast on a nudist
beach, which is different from baring a breast as you take
your lover by the tie and lead the way up stairs with
wiggling hips.

> The very behavior that is often viewed as a constant
> thread running through history and as a powerful
> and primary drive may, in fact, be among the most
> meaning-dependent of all behaviors. It may be among
> the most dependent on extrinsic factors for its capacity
> to motivate or even – perhaps I should say, especially –
> its capacity to pleasure. (William Simon, in Anderson
> (ed.), *The Fontana Post-Modernism Reader*, p. 154)

The industrial revolution, the lip size of our enemies, the
delectations of the emperor . . . I have said that any and
everything has the potential to contribute to the social
context through which we read the body. If I had time, I
could write an encyclopedia charting the ways in which
technological developments, medical knowledge and
economic growth have all contributed to the shifting
social contexts through which we read our sexual meanings. But I haven't got time, so I won't. I do, however,
want to comment upon one particular aspect of the
social context which has a more wide-reaching impact
on our bodies than many others. That is, our bodily
beliefs.

The meanings we make of the body are, to a very large
extent, affected by the beliefs that we hold about the
body. I alluded to this in the sun tans example. In the
1970s and 1980s it was believed that sunshine was good

for us – fresh air, a rich source of vitamin D and so on. Since then our beliefs about the body have changed. Indeed, they are constantly developing. During the 1990s it rose to public awareness that prolonged exposure to the sun causes cancer and premature ageing. As a result, by the turn of the millennium, sun tans had begun to go out of fashion. A bronzed torso had not entirely lost its erotic meaning but it was certainly less sexy than it used to be. Our beliefs about malignant melanomas have changed the context in which the body is read.

Let's take another example. In the days of the Old Testament people were very solemn about testicles. A guy's testicles were almost sacred. They used to swear on the testicles in much the same way that we swear on the Bible today. When a man was making an oath, he would place his hand on the testicles of the man to whom he was making the vow as a sign of his veracity, which is why the word 'testify' has the same root as 'testicle'. In Old Testament times they did not understand that we all begin in the chemistry between the sperm and the egg. They believed that miniature embryos were contained in the semen. What's more it was not understood that spermatozoa are continually being reproduced in the testes. They thought there was a limited number of little humans in a man's testicles that were wasted every time he masturbated. Hence masturbation was a very serious offence indeed. In some instances it was punishable by death. The belief that miniature humans were swimming around in semen greatly affected the meanings that the Israelites made of the body.

Today we believe it is possible to have heterosexual vaginal intercourse without getting pregnant. 'Sex and reproduction have become separated: not only does effective contraception mean that an act of intercourse need have no reproductive consequences, but conception can now occur without intercourse having taken place' (Hall, *Sex, Gender and Social Change in Britain since 1880*, p. 1). This is a belief that is slightly at odds with reality. The British Pregnancy Advisory Service reports that 60 per cent of women requesting abortions claim to have been using contraception when they conceived. Doubtless some of these pregnancies were due to split condoms or forgotten pills, but even when contraception is used correctly there is still a chance of making a baby. If 100 women have sex using a cap and spermicide, then within a year between four and eight will be pregnant. Two will be pregnant within a year using a condom and one will become pregnant using the combined pill. By the time you have allowed for human error in using contraception, it is more accurate to claim that contraception considerably reduces the chances of pregnancy but it does not remove the possibility completely. That is the reality. What is generally believed is another thing. Gays know there's no such thing as safe sex, but the prevailing myth among heterosexuals who don't want babies is that so long as you use contraception you're going to be all right.

As a result of this widely held belief, heterosexual vaginal intercourse is less meaningful than it used to be. Until the 1950s vaginal intercourse was generally used as an expression of lifelong commitment in marriage. The belief that you can have sex without getting pregnant developed some time after the 1960s with the introduction of the pill. By the year 2001, the average age of first

intercourse was 16 for both sexes while the average age
of marriage was 28 for women and 30 for men (National
Survey of Sexual Attitudes and Lifestyles 2000 and
Office for National Statistics). An act of heterosexual
vaginal intercourse in the context of the belief that you
might make a baby takes on a different significance from
the same act in the context of the belief that nothing like
that could ever happen – or if it does you could always
have an abortion.

Implicit in my discussion about meanings has been the
understanding that they do not stand still. It has been
well established in linguistic theory that meanings are
constantly on the move. A trawl through *The Shorter
Oxford English Dictionary* is all it takes to appreciate
that the meanings of words evolve. T. S. Eliot says that
words 'Will not stay still' (*Complete Poems and Plays*,
p. 175), and it's just the same with the meanings we
make of our bodies. Our meanings change as our bodies
change, as our beliefs about our bodies develop, as the
social context through which we read the body changes.

When AIDS came to public awareness at the start of
the 1980s it was very interesting to observe how anal
sex acquired a new gravitas. Our bodies developed a
potential for a fatal disease that was new and as a result
the high-risk anal sex got serious. In his book *Love
Undetectable*, Andrew Sullivan describes an experience
of anal sex that had a meaning it could never have had
before the virus was known. This is how it happened:

As night fell, we found ourselves suddenly, unexpect-
edly in an embrace that lasted for longer than it should
have. The relief of survival, the knowledge of survival

was suddenly all too much. We found ourselves holding each other almost as if we were all each of us had
left and with a need and relish that took both of us by
surprise. There was so much joy in it and so much
sadness that it is difficult to express what it was that
we actually felt, and since it could not be put into
words, we did not put it into words. There are times
when only bodies can express what minds cannot
account for. So we kissed and embraced and clung to
each other in silence. And as the passion grew, we
found ourselves, without a word between us, taking
the embrace still further and further until, for the first
time in each of our lives, as our bodies came together,
we did not bother to reach for protection, and inti-
mated in a single, mutual, liberating smile that not
even the caution of so many years would bring anything any longer between us. 'Are you sure?' he asked
me. 'Yes, I'm sure,' I replied. No other words were
necessary. And the barrier broke at last. And the fear
was rebuked at last. (p. 60)

That act of anal sex had a meaning that was very specific
to that particular time and place in history – the US in the
mid 1990s. Both men were HIV-positive, both had feared
dying before their youth was over, both had lost their
closest friends through AIDS-related illnesses. Shortly
before that sex took place a new cocktail of drugs had
been developed. They were lucky enough to live in a
country in which those drugs were available to them and
had experienced the shocking joy of being told the virus
was no longer detectable in their blood. Both were now
having to renegotiate their way in a world where, unlike

their dear friends, they had the hope of survival. That was why they clung to each other as though they were all they had left. That was why the sex was charged with joy and sadness and why having sex without a condom was so significant to both of them, a way of rebuking the fear at last. That act could not have had the same meaning in the early 1970s before the AIDS virus had been discovered. It would not have meant the same thing in the late 1980s before they had discovered a way of controlling it.

Our sexualities are intricately connected to society. They are woven into culture through a wide, complex variety of ways. The ways in which we get turned on are affected by social class, medical knowledge, conventions about the treatment of children and the roles in which we envisage ourselves in the public world of work. What's more, through the power of association, the body functions as a kind of language that we 'read' according to context. Our turn-ons are therefore affected by everything that makes up our social context, be that economics, technology, religion, law or our beliefs about the way the body works. When we are sexually aroused it feels like a primitive, primeval instinct stirring within us. It is – but it is an instinct that is knitted into everything else in the world.

Chapter Six

What Do We Do with It?

At the start of this book I said sexuality was conceptually tricky. I wasn't wrong, was I?

Through the past three chapters we have arrived at some kind of an understanding of sexuality. We have established that it is rooted in the body and therefore concerns hormones and habits, muscle and memory, nerves and thoughts. We also know that it has got something to do with the unconscious, a drive to survive which is shaped through our babyhood and childhood experiences. As well as that, we have noticed that when we are turned on, we are being aroused not just through the body but through the meanings we make of the body which are derived from any number of different arenas. Sexuality is therefore connected to the wider society, woven into spheres as diverse as economics, technology, medicine, education, law and religion. Sexuality is as physical as hunger, as mental as arithmetic, as unconscious as dreams and as revealing of our history as the British Museum.

And that is about as much as we understand of it. It is not by any means a complete understanding. On the contrary, it's very patchy. All I've said is that sexuality has got something to do with this and something to do with that, but I haven't been able to show how this and that connect up with each other. I'm not alone in being unable to do that. Nobody has accomplished that task, though Freud perhaps came the closest. The precise nature of the relationship between the body and the unconscious and the extent of the role that society plays in our sexual development are not yet known to anyone. We can't explain why one chap turns out to be a boob-man while his brother is repulsed by breasts. I'd really like to know why some childhood experiences 'stick' and become part of our adult sexualities while others just pass us by – but I don't. I have asked what sexuality is. I have given a response, but it is one that has raised as many questions as it has answered.

And we take those questions with us. In this chapter we are rounding a corner. This book opened by asking, 'What is sexuality?' In chapter two I offered a definition and in the following three chapters I analysed different dimensions of sexual arousal and thereby established something of its nature. It's time to move on but it's important to note, as we do, that we haven't managed to suss sexuality yet. As we turn from the 'What is sexuality?' section of this book to the 'What should we be doing with it?' part there is still scope for developing our understanding of this mysterious business of being aroused. The hope is that through living our sexualities well we will be better able to understand them and, through understanding them better, be better able to live them well.

How do we live with this capacity to be aroused? What should we do with it? When should we have sex and when should we decline the offer? How should we behave out on the town and between the sheets? Is it polite to fake orgasms? Should we have a go at everything that turns us on or are there some rules or guidelines to help us work out our sexual behaviour?

In order to answer these questions I am going to engage with Christian tradition. This is important for two reasons. It is important because it is impossible to disentangle Christianity from the British legal system and ways of conceptualizing sex. Any historical understanding of British sexuality involves, to some extent, getting inside the mind of the Church. For Christians there are more personal and pressing reasons for engaging with Christian tradition. Far too many of us have ended up in the position of experiencing our sexualities in conflict with our faith. This is an intensely painful dilemma and one which makes us vulnerable to the temptation of resolving it by either abandoning our spirituality to make way for our sexuality or our sexuality to make way for our spirituality. Neither is a good idea. It is, therefore, as a matter of urgency that we undertake the task of integrating our understanding of God with whatever turns us on.

In chapter one I said the Roman Catholic Church and the Church of England reach the same conclusion about sex, namely that there should be no sex outside marriage. The Catholic Church claims a marriage is not a proper marriage until sex has taken place. It also says contraception should never be used, though since the Second Vatican Council in 1965 it has conceded the rhythm method is an acceptable form of birth control. The Anglican Church permits contraception but says people who marry should be open to the possibility of having children. Since 1991 the Church of England has said that, unless they are priests, men who have sex with men and women who have sex with women, and who do this having seriously weighed the issues involved, should be offered friendship and understanding by the church though they are not in line with the God-given moral order. The conclusions reached by both denominations of the Church are similar. The bigger difference is in the methods through which they reach their conclusions. The Church of England places greater emphasis on the Bible in thinking through its sexual ethics. The Roman Catholic Church bases its teaching on 'natural law, illuminated and enriched by divine revelation' (*Humanae Vitae*, para. 4).

I like the approach of using the Bible as a way of understanding sexuality. As I said in the first chapter, the Bible was written over a period of about twelve centuries from a wide range of different social situations. In *Issues in Human Sexuality* the Church of England bishops draw this out and make the connections between sexuality and its social context. They explain, for example, that the Israelites felt strongly the imperative to go forth, increase and multiply because they were under threat in their territory. There was therefore a need to make babies so that their fathers' names would be preserved in Israel and the family's share of the land held secure. That's another reason why wasting semen through masturbation was taken so seriously and why polygamy and having sex with slave girls were acceptable practices. The Anglican Church is good at making the connections between spirituality and society and the bishops' historical approach to sexuality is one I very much appreciate.

But for all that I appreciate the approach, I do not agree that it says in the Bible there should be no sex outside marriage. The Bible clearly says you should not commit adultery. It is nothing like as clear about sex for the unmarried, whether they be single, lesbian or gay. The text usually cited to support the view that you should wait for your wedding day before having vaginal intercourse is in Matthew's Gospel where Jesus is approached by the teachers of the Law, who are trying to trick him. They ask if it is against the Law for a man to divorce his wife for any reason. Jesus replies:

> Have you not read that the creator from the beginning made them male and female? . . . This is why a man must leave father and mother and cling to his wife and the two become one body? They are no longer two, therefore, but one body. So then, what God has united, man must not divide. (Matthew 19.5)

The bishops say it is not unreasonable to infer from this that Jesus 'regarded heterosexual love as the God-given pattern' (*Issue in Human Sexuality*, 2.17). Others say this text shows that gays should be celibate and that men should be manly and women should be feminine and do what they're told.

I disagree with all of these inferences. I don't think Jesus was talking about sex, gender complementarity or even marriage as such. He was talking about divorce and in his day divorce was a one-way street. It was only the man that could issue the writ of divorce and when he did it meant a woman was left destitute with no money, no status and a shame so intense no other man would want her. The teachers of the Law asked Jesus if it was ever right for men to do this. Jesus replied to the men of the book in the terms they would understand – he quoted Genesis and said, 'No way'.

The Bible doesn't actually have a lot to say about sexuality, probably because sexuality is a relatively recent invention. It is much more concerned with justice to the poor than with masturbation, living together and 'the gay issue'. The problem with coming to the Bible with our contemporary sexual dilemmas is that the material is so scant it makes the margins for interpretation very wide indeed. I think the bishops interpret the Bible from the perspective of happily married men whereas I interpret it as a feminist claiming Jesus as my ally. The bishops say there is in Scripture 'an evolving convergence on the ideal of lifelong, monogamous, heterosexual union as the setting intended by God for the proper development of men and women as sexual beings' (*Issues in Human Sexuality*, 2.29). When I read the Gospels I see a man who never married and never initiated any teaching on marriage, standing beside women who had had more than one sexual partner and telling his disciples to leave their families to follow him. We cannot say categorically that the Bible says there is to be no sex outside marriage. That is one interpretation, and it is a reasonable one. There are others.

The Roman Catholic Church has a different approach. In *Familiaris Consortio* Pope John Paul II suggests an understanding of sex similar to the one I outlined in the previous chapter. He intimates that it is a kind of language. In the passage I quoted in chapter one, he says sexuality concerns the innermost being of man and woman and is realized in a truly human way only if it is

an integral part of the love in which they commit themselves totally to one another until death. 'The total physical self-giving would be a lie if it were not the sign
and fruit of a total personal self-giving,' he says (para.
11). In other words sex has a meaning, namely the total,
personal, giving of self. It also 'represents the mystery of
Christ's incarnation and the mystery of his covenant'
(para. 13).

I warm very much to the idea of sex as a language. As
I showed in the last chapter, it is irrefutable that sex is a
means of communication and that meanings and context
have a large role to play in our being turned on. In
general, what I appreciate about the Catholic Church is
the way it makes the connections between inner life and
outer life, the mirroring between the personal self-giving
and the physical self-giving. When it manages to communicate a sense of word made flesh, body made sacred
and a world 'charged with the grandeur of God' (Gerard
Manley Hopkins, 'God's Grandeur', in Hamilton (ed.),
Gerard Manley Hopkins: Selected Poems) it reaches
deeper into the places from which the erotic juices flow
than Hugh Hefner and his Playboy empire ever could.

My quarrel with the Catholic Church is not with the
notion that sex has a meaning. It is with the implication
that the meaning is fixed. The Pope is saying that sex
means 'a total personal giving' regardless of the context
and the intention of the people concerned. He is saying
that meaning does not change with time and it does not
change as our knowledge of the body changes. Sex
means what God made it to mean, full stop.

I understand why the Catholic Church takes this view
of meanings. The early church was influenced by Greek

philosophies – Platonism, which claimed that meanings are objective, independent, real, divine and changeless, and Stoicism, which claimed there was an impartial, inevitable, moral order of the universe. Its teaching about sex was developed through thinking on natural law, a medieval concept arising from a world view which claimed everything was made by God for a reason. The idea was that by appreciating the function of a part of the body you could understand how God had intended it to be used and so to use it accordingly was to be in line with its God-given character. The church therefore claims the meaning of sex is inherent in its nature. It follows that if you do it without meaning what the act objectively does mean, you're telling a fib. This is coherent. It makes sense.

But this way of thinking only works if you believe there are such things as inherent meanings. It does not work if you take the view, well established throughout the twentieth century, that meanings are not independent, changeless entities dangling in the stratosphere or contained in the semen. It does not work if you appreciate that social contexts change and our bodies change and our beliefs about our bodies change and that the meanings we make of them alter accordingly. Semen is necessary for making babies, says Thomas Aquinas in a passage I quoted in chapter one. Making babies is therefore what semen is for; to spill semen without making babies is therefore against natural law and, if this is done on purpose, is a sin. Can we not just as easily argue that the clitoris is necessary for a woman's orgasm; having an orgasm is therefore what the clitoris is for; to turn a woman on without giving her an orgasm is therefore against natural law and, if this is done on purpose, is a sin? The meaning of heterosexual vaginal intercourse is not fixed. It changes as everything else in the world changes. For a man to have vaginal intercourse with his slave girl in 1003 BC means something different from a man having vaginal intercourse with his au pair in AD 2003.

I disagree with the Roman Catholic Church when it claims that the meaning of sex is inherent in its nature. That does not mean, however, that I go so far as to say vaginal intercourse could mean anything. My claim is that there is a complex relationship between the body and the meanings that we make of it. I do not think the meaning of vaginal intercourse is fixed but neither do I think that the meanings we make of it are arbitrary. Heterosexual vaginal intercourse is the way we make babies and that fact has an enormous role to play in the significance we attribute to it. Shaking hands, for example, is a good way of communicating: 'Hello, nice to meet you'; 'Let's be friends'; or, 'It's a deal'. That's because as a gesture, it is quick, it does not involve taking our clothes off, and has few physical ramifications. Could we just as easily use vaginal intercourse, rather than hand-shaking, as a way of doing business or greeting strangers? Of course not. There would be chaos, disease, unwanted pregnancies and no time to do anything else if we had a convention whereby we shagged every person we met as a sign of politeness. By the same argument, there is a very good reason why vaginal intercourse, rather than hand-shaking, has historically been used as a symbol of marriage, namely that it is through vaginal intercourse that we procreate.

My quibble with the Church is a small but significant one. The Church says that the meaning of vaginal intercourse is inherent in its nature. I am saying that there is a range of meanings that we can make of vaginal intercourse and that those meanings are constrained by its nature. The Church is saying that God made the meaning. I am saying that we make the meanings. The Church is saying that vaginal intercourse objectively does mean 'total personal self-giving'. I am saying that we can use vaginal intercourse to communicate 'total personal self-giving' if we set about it with that intention. When people decide to share vaginal intercourse with the person they marry and nobody else, then it will inevitably be a sign of the uniqueness of their relationship. We could, of course, use kissing, sharing orgasms or holding hands as a sign of the exclusiveness of marriage and in some cultures that is indeed what they do. However, heterosexual vaginal intercourse, while by no means the only form of sex, is a particularly apt way of symbolizing a relationship into which children are welcome because it is the way we make babies. For those who know that marriage and children are what they want one day there is a lot of sense in reserving vaginal intercourse so it can be used to express that commitment.

I have always felt ambivalent about marriage, so it is not quite accurate to say that I saved vaginal intercourse for then. However, because it is the way we make babies, I have never felt able to have vaginal intercourse in relationships in which I felt fear rather than joy at the prospect that the condom might just burst. Through a mixture of choice and circumstance, this meant the only person with whom I have shared vaginal intercourse has been the man that I did eventually marry. I think there is a great deal to recommend about this. It meant that through my decades of being single I had no fear of unwanted pregnancies, minimal risk of disease and some glorious woman-centred sex along the way. It also meant that when I did marry I had a way of being with my partner that I had not experienced with anybody else before. I enjoy that.

We can use our bodies to say to somebody: 'I am going to invite you to a place inside me where nobody else has ever been before,' or 'I want to offer myself to you in a way I have never offered myself to anybody else before.' If you say that only to the person you marry then you can carry on saying that and celebrating that every time you do it for the rest of your lives. It's not fibbing to have vaginal intercourse with a lot of people, but it is limiting. It limits the way in which we can use the body to communicate, 'Only for you'. That meaning is no less real for the fact it is chosen.

But having said that (though that's saying quite a lot) it is not on the issue of sex outside marriage that my main quarrel with the Church lies. I do not think it is adequate merely to replace 'no sex outside marriage because that's what it says in the Bible', or 'no sex outside marriage because that would be telling a fib', with 'no sex outside marriage because that's the way to get the most out of heterosexual vaginal intercourse'. My bone of contention with the Church and with British society in general is more radical. I disagree with the way in which sex is conceptualized right from the start.

My quarrel with the Church, for all that it offers a more holistic view of sexuality than many institutions, is that it tends to think of sex in terms of an act – 'full physical sexual relations' as the bishops euphemistically put it (*Issues in Human Sexuality*, 3.14). This is echoed by the rest of society. It is not uncommon to hear a penis in a vagina described as 'the sex act' and penises in mouths and anuses as 'other sexual acts'. It's because sex has been characterized as an act for so many centuries that lesbians have to put up with men saying, 'I hope you don't mind me asking, but what exactly do you do?' In the sixth century the church had manuals called 'Penitentials' which provided lists of sexual acts like oral sex, anal sex and certain positions for vaginal intercourse, and prescribed the appropriate penance for each one. Even today a penis in a vagina is considered good if you are married, a penis in an anus is considered bad whatever the circumstances, and a finger stimulating the clitoris and giving an earth-shaking orgasm isn't really considered to be sex at all. In England and Wales it is illegal for a man to have anal sex with a woman. It doesn't matter whether she consented or whether they enjoyed it. Anal intercourse is deemed to be wrong by the very nature of the act. Until 1991 a man was entitled to have vaginal intercourse with his wife. It didn't matter whether she consented or whether she begged him to stop. Marital vaginal intercourse was deemed to be right by the very nature of the act. We need to move on from this way of thinking. I am not saying that acts are insignificant. On the contrary, in both this chapter and the last I have explained how a sexual act can be enormously meaningful. But I am saying that you cannot judge sex by the act alone. When we conceptualize sex as an act, sexual ethics tends to revolve around what

bit goes up what orifice rather than the quality of the
relationship and the love that is made.

The other problem with an act-orientated sexual ethic
is that it isn't very practical. Many of the dilemmas that
trouble us on a daily basis have got nothing to do with
sexual acts themselves. How does the 'no sex before
marriage' edict help people who have sadomasochistic
dynamics in their sexualities and want to know if it's a
good idea to act out their fantasies with their partners?
What does it have to offer when one person in a partner-
ship wants to have sex a lot more than the other? How
does it enable us to make sense of the times when we are
aroused by things other than people? Can it guide us
when our partner can only get turned on through acting
out fantasies that are rooted in childhood abuse? Does it
help us know how to behave when we are in a committed monogamous relationship with one person but are
conscious of turning another person on in a no-touching-
fully-clothed kind of way? These are the kind of everyday questions to which we need to work out answers and
to which 'no sex before marriage' has very little to say.

I think we need to think of sex not in terms of acts but
in terms of whatever turns us on. We need to work out
how to be loving, creative and responsible with our
capacity to be aroused and with our capacity to arouse
another. Sex is not just vaginal intercourse. That is a
sexist definition of sex, as Shere Hite has demonstrated.
Sex is kissing on the lips, running fingers down the spine,
biting buttocks, clamping nipples and smelling menstrual
blood. It is wearing thongs, wearing nothing, wearing
leather, tickling all over, whipping and licking, spanking
and wanking. Sex is whispering fantasies. It is sucking

toes, sucking breasts, sucking penises and tasting semen, vibrating on the clitoris, going deep, deep into the arse-hole, eating the vulva and tasting its juices, holding each other in silent, foetal moments. Sex is all of these things and many, many more.

In the heart of the Bible, in Matthew's Gospel to be precise, the same teachers of the Law ask Jesus another question to catch him out – 'Master which is the greatest commandment of the Law?' Jesus replies:

> You must love the Lord your God with all your heart, with all your soul, and with all your mind. The second resembles it: You must love your neighbour as your-self. On these two commandments hang the whole Law, and the Prophets also. (Matthew 22.36–40)

I don't think we take these words of Jesus seriously enough. Jesus is saying that all the legalism in Leviticus, all the pouting of the prophets, all the rumpus in Romans boils down to these three things – love God, love your neighbour, love yourself. Surely that must be our starting point when it comes to thinking out how to live our sexualities well.

During the communion service there is a point at which the priest addresses the congregation and says: 'We are the body of Christ. In the one Spirit we were all baptized into one body. Let us then pursue all that makes for peace and builds up the common life.' Our vicar, who's a bit irrepressible, likes to improvise at that point. He often says something like: 'Let us then pursue all that makes for love and joy and peace and justice and every-thing good that we share together.' Whenever he comes out with a new one, I have the same thought: 'What does that mean in terms of our capacity to get turned on? Here we are a sexual people, a people who juice and yearn and touch and swell. How can we use our sexualities to pursue all that makes for love and joy and peace and justice and everything good that we share together?'

That is how I am framing the question.

Chapter Seven

Love Yourself

Love yourself.

What would happen if we really loved our sexualities? What would it mean if we looked right deep down into the belly of our being and said 'I love you' to that part of ourselves which moistens and yearns and swells? What would we be like if we were completely at ease with ourselves as sexual beings? How would we be, both within ourselves and in relation to others? That is what this chapter is about.

It's interesting to note the first thoughts that come to mind when I suggest we love ourselves sexually. Some people imagine I am talking about masturbating. Others suppose I am advocating orgies. 'Cop-out' was the response of one person when I said loving ourselves, loving our neighbour and loving the Lord our God should be the basis of our sexual ethics. The assumption is that loving ourselves sexually means indulging in rampant sex with whoever we fancy.

I don't think loving our sexualities means having lots more sex – though it might do and if that is our first thought then it's worth asking ourselves why. It might also mean having less. The average man has had four sexual partners over the past five years and the average woman has had two, according to the *National Survey of Sexual Attitudes and Lifestyles* 2000 (*The Lancet*, 1 December 2001). In the same period, 1 in 12 men and 1 in 28 women have had more than ten sexual partners. Can we deduce from this that we are sexually liberated and having so much more fun than we used to in the days when intercourse outside marriage was taboo? Not necessarily. The researchers also discovered that four out of five women who had had intercourse for the first time aged 13 or 14 regretted it. Two out of five young men expressed the same feelings. Even when women had waited until they were aged between 18 and 24 to have their first intercourse, one in five regretted it.

This research concurs with the findings of John Tripp, a consultant paediatrician and senior lecturer in child health at Exeter University who has devised a sex education programme used in secondary schools. 'It is tragic how few girls actually enjoy their first sexual experience,' he says (*Observer*, 15 October 2000). Jo Adams of the Sheffield Centre of Aids and Sexual Health agrees. When she asked teenage girls their reasons for their first intercourse, they said things like: 'to keep my boyfriend', 'to get a cuddle', 'because I loved him', 'to know I'm attractive', 'to get a lift home' (*Observer*, 15 October 2000).

These answers make me wince. I wish I couldn't relate to them but I can. Once I slept in the same bed as a man I didn't fancy and endured being fondled by him. Why? Because he had taken me out for a meal and that had made me feel I owed him something. I'm ashamed to say I was 25 when that happened. Some people never grow out of doing that sort of thing. Sadly, I understand what's going on when teenage girls have intercourse when what they really want is something else. I also understand that once you've lost sight of your body's worth, it becomes all the harder to reclaim it. 'You don't find out that you're attractive, intelligent or beloved in the back seat of a car or in rapid, fumbling sex behind the youth centre,' says Adams. 'Girls can get into a downward spiral of self-esteem and diminishing returns' (*Observer*, 15 October 2000) How true.

Is it different for boys? I would guess so. Certainly I don't find myself wincing in recognition at the things boys say about their first experiences of intercourse. Boys don't have sex as a way of getting a lift home, but they make it clear impressing their friends is a motivating factor. Adams says many boys develop a tough, swaggering public persona as a strategy for hiding their scared, unready, private feelings in the midst of a bullying, homophobic playground culture:

> Boys present a cool and streetwise image, effing and blinding and talking about girls being up for it. Conquest is part of their status. I've heard teenage boys say: 'What's the matter with you? Haven't you got a kid yet? Some kind of poofter?' The way they talk you'd think they were Warren Beatty, but we get them to write down in private the questions they want asked and these great strapping lads of 15 and 16 ask: 'Is it alright to have wet dreams? Or how long should an erect penis be?' (*Observer*, 15 October 2000)

Loving our sexualities does not mean having sex with whoever we can. It means taking care of ourselves. It means taking responsibility for ourselves. If we really loved ourselves we would not have the kind of sex where we wake up in the morning and think, 'Oh no, what have I done?' We would not allow ourselves to get into situations where we are treated carelessly. We would not put ourselves at undue risk of disease or making a baby in circumstances where to do so would be a disaster. If we loved ourselves we would be able to ask for sex when we wanted it and we would be able to bear with the vulnerability that that invitation engenders. We would not retreat from that vulnerability into aggression, denial or manipulative behaviour. If we loved ourselves we would know that it is all right to stop sexual activity at any stage. We would not fake orgasms nor worry about penis size. We would not see sex as conquest or performance. We would not see our masculinity or femininity as something that needed to be proved. If we loved ourselves we would not worry about whether or not we were normal. We would honour our sexualities in all of their waxing and waning, their many moods and seasons, their comforting familiarity and their unknown, adventuring potential.

I would hazard a guess that we all have aspects of our sexuality that we wish were other than they are – the priest who gets turned on through being called a little slut, the lover who can't sustain an erection, the High Court judge who likes to bend over for a spanking, the young woman who is turned on by the breasts of her teacher, the man who is aroused by his cat, the feminist who fantasizes about rape, the guy who goes out cruising though he knows it hurts the man he loves, the husband who comes too quickly and the wife who cannot come at all . . . Have any of us not wished from time to time, or even most of the time, that our sexualities are other than they are?

Our default position about our sexualities tends to be shame. When we are sexually rejected, we feel shame. When we notice our sexualities don't seem to be the same as other people's, we feel shame. When my friend had an orgasm from seeing a church between two layers of Alpine mist, she didn't tell anyone because she felt too ashamed. When an adult abuses a child it can take decades before the survivor is able to feel anger. Until he does, he feels shame. And yet the fact of our sexualities is that whatever they are, whatever their style, whatever the source or cause of our turn-ons, it isn't our fault. Our sexualities are, for the most part, fully developed by the time we emerge from puberty and there wasn't a lot we could have done about them along the way. We are not responsible for the bodies with which we were born, for the way in which our libidos separated, for our childhoods, or for the society which shaped and formed us. There is no point in beating ourselves up about our sexualities, however unusual or antisocial. We had no capacity to control the process through which they came to be.

There is a paradox at work here. I have said that loving our sexualities means taking responsibility for them. I have also said it means recognizing we were not responsible for the things that happened to make us into the sexual adults we are today. There is an emotional logic to those statements for all their seeming contradiction. I believe that as adults we are entirely responsible for the ways we treat other people. That is the subject of my next chapter. However, I also believe that taking responsibility for our sexualities involves 'owning' them, claiming our capacity to be aroused, acknowledging our patterns, accepting these are the ways in which we get turned on. If we don't do this, if we try, in our shame, to suppress and ignore our sexualities we are more likely to end up being careless with that part of ourselves and cause other people to suffer as a result. The paradox is that taking responsibility for our sexualities involves reckoning with the truth that we weren't responsible for the ways in which they came to be. 'Whatever your unique measure and mix of sexuality be very glad,' says the Anglican priest and writer Jim Cotter (*Prayer at Night*, p. 73). I think that is good advice. I do hope we will get there. But we need to work with the less ambitious suggestion first: 'Whatever your unique measure and mix of sexuality – remember it isn't your fault.'

Wendy Maltz, a US sex therapist, tells the story of Joann, a woman whose sexuality was such that she got turned on through fantasies of anal rape. She did not want sex very often but when she did she would manipulate the lovemaking with her husband Tim in such a way as to encourage him to have forceful anal sex with her. This would invariably conclude with Joann curled in a ball on the bed sobbing. Even though Joann was turned on by the anal sex she felt desperately lonely and undermined when she had her fantasies acted out. Her fantasies, which she had been having since she was ten years old, were rooted in the times as a child when her father would spank her in a sexual manner and then penetrate her anally with his finger as he masturbated (*www.top-education.com/Therapies/sextherapy1.htm*).

'Whatever your unique measure and mix of sexuality – remember it isn't your fault.' I wouldn't underestimate the courage it takes for some of us just to get that far.

Loving our sexualities is a costly business and it is more costly for some than for others. It is easier to be glad about your sexuality if you have been cherished all your life than it is if you have been raped or abused as a child. It is easier to accept your sexuality if you can use it to bring your partner pleasure than it is if your relationship is being damaged through incompatible sexual needs. It is easier to be happy about your sexuality if you live in a world which affirms its normality than one which constantly puts out the message you are perverted and sick.

But though it is undoubtedly harder for some than for others, I believe the journey we each have to make is essentially the same. We are all wounded. We are all vulnerable in matters of the groin. No one has a perfect body. There is no such thing as an ideal childhood. We have all been brought up in a world in which power is wielded by some to the detriment of others. 'It would be ahistorical and naïve to imagine that *anyone's* eroticism in this culture could be untouched by this dynamic,' say the US feminists Beverly Wildung Harrison and Carter Heyward (in Nelson and Longfellow (eds), *Sexuality and the Sacred*, p. 133). Heterosexual, toe-sexual, tit-sexual, homosexual, intellectual-sexual, out-of-my-reach-sexual, SM-sexual, or seemingly asexual – we all stand in the same place, the place of needing to say: 'This is my sexuality. I don't know exactly how it came to be, but however it was, it wasn't my fault. It's now up to me to use it well.'

Sooner or later, as we move on in loving our sexualities, a question emerges. Can we change them? It is one thing to recognize we were not responsible for our sexualities as they developed through our growing up, but can we, as adults, intervene in our sexual becoming and change what turns us on? Can Joann do anything about her sexuality, or does she have to accept that being turned on by fantasies of anal rape is just the way it is going to be from now on? Can a chap who gets off on dressing up as a woman transform himself into a regular kind of guy who just likes the missionary position? Can a woman who falls in love with other women get herself emotionally and sexually engaged with a guy? Can someone who hasn't had a randy feeling for years find a switch inside and turn it on? When does loving our sexualities mean accepting them just as they are and when does it mean consciously trying to change them for the better? Can we – and should we – try to alter the ways in which we get turned on?

This is a very important question, but it is too bald to answer as it stands. Whether we can change our sexualities or not depends on which of the many complex means through which they came to be we are trying to affect. If a man is trying to alter an unsatisfactorily low libido it makes a considerable difference if his problem is due to lack of testosterone, childhood trauma or unresolved anger towards his present partner. Sometimes changing our sexualities is as simple as taking Viagra. In other instances it can involve going for psychoanalysis five times a week and still being no further forward.

Joann did manage to change her sexuality with the help of her therapist, Maltz. Like many who work with

survivors of sexual abuse, Maltz claims that it is possible
for those who have been damaged in childhood to find
healing and change the pattern of the ways in which we
get turned on. She says:

> Sexual healing can take several months to several
> years, or more, to accomplish . . . There are different
> levels of sexual healing work that a survivor can
> pursue . . .You *can* repair the damage done to you in
> the past. You can look forward to a new surge of self-
> respect, personal contentment, emotional intimacy.
> When you reclaim your sexuality, you reclaim your-
> self. (*www.healthysex.com/saharticle.html*)

Relate, which has a psychosexual therapy service, claims
that when they did research on 1,000 couples, 82 per
cent of both men and women who completed the therapy
said their sexual relationship was now closer to or very
much what they would want it to be (*www.relate.org.
uk/press_pages.pst.html*). Likewise Haas and Haas claim
that most couples at some stage will have sexual problems
of one kind of another. While acknowledging that sexual
difficulties can be resistant to treatment and that figures
for its effectiveness are very difficult to collate, they conclude: 'It is probable, however, that most people who
work diligently with a *competent* therapist and stay in
treatment can look forward to significant improvement
and great satisfaction' (*Understanding Sexuality*, p. 513).

Freud, on the other hand, was certainly not optimistic
about the possibility of a homosexual changing his
'object choice' as he called it. 'In actual numbers, the
successes achieved by psychoanalytic treatment of . . .

homosexuality . . . are not very striking . . . In general to undertake to convert a fully developed homosexual into a heterosexual is not much more promising than to do the reverse' (*Case Histories II*, p. 376). Nothing that we have discovered since Freud has disproved this theory. Some people try, of course, and there are therapists who claim a success rate of 30 per cent with the most highly motivated of clients (*www.indegay/forum.org/articles/ sullivan1.html*). However, you also have to examine what such therapists define as 'success'. Andrew Sullivan reveals an example of a man who was said to be 'cured' of his homosexuality by psychotherapist Steven Richfield:

> I've come to accept that there is a homosexual part inside of me that I may never be able to get rid of but maybe I can learn to live with it. The other day I was at the swim club with my wife and sons. A man in a very tight bathing suit walked by and I caught myself staring and beginning to have fantasies. But just as quickly I stopped myself, told myself it was not such a big deal, and dove into the water. And it didn't ruin my day. (*Love Undetectable*, p. 166)

When you consider that that is cited by Richfield as an example of therapy that worked, Freud's summation of the situation seems to be the better one.

The decision to enter into therapy in an attempt to change your sexuality is a big one that should not be undertaken lightly. Changing your sexuality through hormone therapy is one thing. Going back over an experience of overwhelming terror with a view to re-emerging from it in a different way is another. There is always the possibility you will make your sexuality worse. The psychotherapist Robert Akeret tells a salutary tale. In *The Man who Loved a Polar Bear* he writes about a client called Charles who had fallen in love with a polar bear called Zero at the circus where he worked. Charles ended up in therapy because whenever he tried to have sex with Zero she thumped him about the head and nearly killed him. Through Akeret's help Charles came to understand the danger he was in and he left the circus to save his life. When Akeret met Charles nearly 30 years later he had become a lecturer in circus skills by day and was a whipping boy for a pair of dominatrices by night. This pained Akeret, not because he was troubled by SM in itself, but because there had been no sadomasochistic dynamic in Charles' sexuality when he was in love with the polar bear.

> These S-M games were a substitute for the feelings Charles could not permit himself: his 'bestial' love of Zero (p. 98) . . . There is a distinct possibility that it was therapy itself that . . . robbed Charles of his strongest and deepest feelings, robbed him of feelings in the name of personal survival. (p. 228)

Given that the journey is risky, how do we decide whether to attempt to change our sexualities or not? In my opinion we should never attempt to change the way in which we get turned on because of some ill-considered notion of what it means to be normal. We should not hold in our heads an idea of what an 'ideal' sexuality would be like and try to manoeuvre our own so that it lives up to that. That would be to diminish the glorious, generous, abundant, effervescent, spurting-through-the-universe sexuality of God.

What would constitute a 'perfect' sexuality anyway? If we were 'without sin', what would our sexualities be like? Would we be more randy or less? Would we be only attracted to people of the other sex or would we be able to respond lovingly and erotically to men and women alike? Would our sexualities be softer and sweeter, or would we be better able to embrace the darker, more animal sides of ourselves? Would the range of things that turn us on be narrower or would we be more flexible, more open, more able to be aroused through a diverse number of things, people and situations? I find these intriguing questions but I have no idea what the answers are. All I can say with any certainty is that in a 'perfect' world, our sexualities would all be different from each other's. We all have different bodies, different child-hoods, different minds, different cultures, different ways of making sense of the world. In everything from our physicalities to our musicalities to our spiritualities we are a people of infinite variety. Why should we expect to be roughly homogenous when it comes to sex?

The sex therapist Wendy Maltz has considerably more helpful criteria. She says the questions we need to ask are not about the things that turn us on, but about the effect that those things have on us and on other people. She says we need to ask if the experience of being turned on increases or decreases our self-esteem. We need to ask whether it causes harm emotionally or physically either to ourselves or to other people. We need to ask if our fantasies trigger abusive or compulsive sex. We need to assess if we can use our sexualities to draw close to other

people or if they get in the way of emotional intimacy
and leave us feeling frightened, ashamed and isolated
(*www.healthysex.com/hierarchy*).

In the last chapter I said you cannot judge sex by the
act alone. We can see this very clearly in thinking about
Joann, for whom anal sex left her curled up in a ball on
the bed sobbing. Other people experience it differently:
'I felt like a fresh virgin all over again,' said one man of
being penetrated anally by his partner's finger. 'It's
something that I'll never forget. It was very different
from a penis-orientated orgasm, came from a deeper, different place. Strange and beautiful' (*The Hite Report
on Male Sexuality*, p. 574). Another said: 'Anal intercourse is a feeling of fullness, warmth, being possessed,
cuddled, explored, manipulated, loved, used, needed
and surrounding another man with your own warmth,
love, usefulness and needs' (Hite, p. 578). The questions
we should be asking of our sexualities are not whether
they are normal or even what God intended, but whether
we can use them to make love grow.

I would therefore like to pay tribute to two kinds of
bravery. One is the bravery of those who decide to
change their sexualities, who enter into their deepest and
most Oedipal of moments, who revisit the points of their
distress, who go down a dark path into the most shad-
owy, shameful parts of themselves in the hope of being
transformed into freer, happier and more complete
people. To them I say: 'You are heroes. You are Good
Friday people. You are pioneers of the way. I salute you.'
But there are other people I salute too. They are the ones
who decide to come to terms with their sexualities just as
they are, the ones who say: 'For whatever reason, this is

the sexuality that I have right now and I'm going to get out there and love with it anyway.'

I have already said that I have a scar in my central nervous system that sometimes causes messages between my brain and the lower half of my body to be blocked. When I was first diagnosed with multiple sclerosis I spent a lot of time considering its origins. Was I born with that vulnerability? Was there something about my childhood experiences that exasperated the condition? Was it caused by something in the environment like the mercury of my dental fillings, the chlorine and nitrates in tap water, or radar waves in the 10 cm waveband of microwave ovens? Who knows? I certainly don't. I have asked those questions but I have not had any answers and, after a while, the question of where that scar came from is far less important than the question of how I can live with it right now in a loving and creative way. How did my sexuality come to be? I don't know, and I have reached a point at which that is no longer the important question. It's much more important that I learn how to love with it.

John, the Gospel-writer, tells us that after Jesus had been crucified he rose from the dead and appeared to his disciples in a bodily form. Even though he had risen, even though he had passed through death and out the other side, he still bore the marks of his wounds – the nails in his hands and the spear in his side (John 20.19–29). 'Those dear tokens of his passion/Still his dazzling body bears,' say the eighteenth-century hymn-writers Wesley and Cennick (*English Hymnal*, 7). To me this is an image of what we can all become when we learn to love ourselves, sexualities and all. We don't lose the marks of our wounds but they do not stop us dazzling.

So far in this chapter I have been thinking about loving ourselves specifically in terms of our sexualities. I have been focusing on coming to terms with and taking responsibility for the ways in which we get turned on. But our sexualities don't exist in isolation. They are intricately connected to the rest of our beings, indeed to the rest of the universe. If our love of our sexualities is to be complete, it must be supported by love for everything else about us.

I have no idea whether this is a universal phenomenon or not but I have noticed that my sexuality is intertwined with what I would call my unlived life. By that I mean that when there are desires I have ignored or needs I have suppressed, these often make themselves known to me in the form of a persistent and insistent yearning for someone that personifies that unlived part of myself. I might find, for example, that I get into a can't eat, can't sleep, biting-my-own-arm-off kind of desire for a rugged, earthy, man with a big beard and dirt under his finger nails. One way of dealing with that yearning is to have sex with him, but in my experience that very often isn't possible either because he's in a committed relationship with someone else or I'm in a committed relationship with someone else or he doesn't fancy me. There is another way of dealing with that desire which is to ask a question: 'What do I need to embrace so that I might be at peace?' If I ask my libido that, I might find that what is turning me on about this man is his life which is rooted in the seasons and the elements while I have been stuck at my computer working with words for far too many years.

What I need is to smell the blossom, dig the garden and put my own hands into soil. When I claim that part of myself for myself the yearning for the person who revealed it to me either goes completely or becomes a gentle appreciation rather than a desperate, all-consuming desire.

I am not saying this is easy. I am certainly not saying that I have found a fail-safe technique for dealing with each of our wanton turn-ons. But I am saying that to take care of ourselves sexually involves taking care of every part of ourselves. I think people who understand this are those who are able to live a dynamic and creative style of celibacy. When I got married, contained in my vows was the promise never to have sex with anyone other than my husband for as long as we both lived. I see that as a commitment to myself as much as to God and to my partner. My capacity to keep that promise depends on the extent to which I ensure I am living out my calling. If I don't attend to the part of myself that wants to make music then sooner or later I'll want to shag a musician. If I don't come to terms with ageing as it is happening day by day, then I'm vulnerable to having a mid-life crisis in which I want to run off with a toy boy.

In Buddhism there are five principles for leading an ethical life. A community known as the Friends of the Western Buddhist Order, which is concerned with making the truths of Buddhism available to the West, expresses these precepts both negatively and positively, in terms of what you should move away from and in terms of what you should work towards. Buddhists are urged to move away from false speech and move towards truthful communication; to move away from taking what is not given and move towards practising generosity; to move away from harming living things and move towards doing acts of loving kindness; to move away from intoxication and move towards mindfulness; to move away from sexual misconduct and move towards. . . Now that is an interesting one. What would you imagine the opposite of sexual misconduct was? Chastity, perhaps? Suppression of desire? No. According to the precept the opposite of sexual misconduct is contentment. There is profound wisdom in that.

Loving our sexualities means loving our bodies in all their strength and fragility, their sweating and moistening, their filling and depleting, their ageing and developing, our private parts and public faces, our greying hairs and breaking voices, our memories and our cellulite, our thoughts and our testicles, our smiles, our bleeding wombs. Loving our sexualities means loving the unconscious, honouring its processes and attending to our dreams, respecting what is hidden as much as what is seen, delighting in shadow and reason, in darkness and light. Loving our sexualities means loving our childhoods, cherishing our former selves, acknowledging with gratitude those who helped us to grow and daring to forgive those whose wounds we still bear. Loving our sexualities means loving our world, recognizing that we are who we are because of those who have gone before us, acknowledging that we in turn are shaping the sexualities of those that are to come.

Loving our sexualities, far from being the cop-out that my friend imagines, is actually something we will never fully achieve in this lifetime. It is something a 13-year-old lad in a bullying playground can only begin to do.

Whatever our stage of life the work of loving ourselves goes on. 'Love yourself' is a dynamic commandment calling us deeper and deeper into our sexualities, uncovering new layers, revealing fresh truths, drawing us ever on in our capacity to be turned on.

One night a lover turned to me and said, 'May I congratulate you on your glorious sexuality?' Yes, you may. You may bow down before my awesome, mysterious body and my clear, original mind; you may honour my story, be tender with my wounds, cherish my yearnings and unspoken dreams; you may pay homage to my magical juicings and pungent smells, the secret caverns and magnificent connections of my resplendent sexuality. Please do.

Love yourself.

Chapter Eight

Love Your Neighbour

In 1999 Simon Thomas, aged 32, was convicted for possessing 7,000 images of child pornography. He said:

> I have suffered from an unnatural interest in images of children since about the age of 14. I use the term 'suffered' quite deliberately. Has [*Daily Mail* columnist] Lynda Lee-Potter spent more than half her life hating the person she sees every time she looks in a mirror? I have. I couldn't even get help; after all, if I hated myself because of my problem, how would other people look at me if they found out? Fear of hatred, persecution and ostracism can stop you from achieving something you want more than anything else. I was left to fight this problem on my own for nearly 18 years. (*Daily Mail*, 27 July 2000)

Eventually Thomas tried to commit suicide. It was only when he was in a psychiatric ward, having lost nearly two-thirds of the blood in his body, that he was able to tell a psychiatrist why he wanted to die. He co-operated in a subsequent police investigation, pleaded guilty and was sentenced to four months' imprisonment for possessing indecent photographs of children. Thomas is now beginning to understand the cause of his sexuality and it is beginning to change through working with professionals over an extended period. He says:

> I finally spilled it out to a psychiatrist expecting disgust and hatred. Even now it confuses me that I didn't receive that reaction then and never have since. Not from the professionals who helped me put my mind back together after the suicide attempt and who are now helping me fix the underlying problem. Nor from the family and friends who have all stood by me and supported me once they learned the truth. (*Daily Mail*, 27 July 2000)

In the previous chapter I talked about learning to love ourselves. I said this meant recognizing that our sexualities are not our fault. If we understand that, if we have really done that work of visiting our own painful and frozen places, if we have looked right deep down into the belly of our own beings and understood that we did not control the processes through which our sexualities came to be, then there will be an inevitable corollary – compassion.

Loving our neighbour as we love ourselves does not in any way mean sex offenders should not be brought to justice. Of course they should. It does not mean feeling no anger or disgust at those who use their sexualities to bring others distress. When I've been working through my feelings about sexual abuse I've had some pretty violent fantasies concerning testicles and carving knives. But if we really love ourselves, if we have done that tough, tough work of accepting the dark and incongruous parts of our own sexualities, we will find we no longer need to create a distance between ourselves and our neighbour. We will not say of other people: 'They're sick, I'm normal. They're beyond the pale, I'm within the bounds of social acceptability. They're the scum of the earth, I'm all right Jack.'

I spent the whole of the last chapter on the theme of loving yourself. I make no apology for that. Unless we have begun the work of loving ourselves, we don't stand a chance of loving our neighbour. If we haven't taken responsibility for our own sexualities then somebody somewhere will suffer the fall-out from that one day. Loving ourselves and loving our neighbour are not two separate processes but are all part of the same dynamic.

What else would it mean if we loved our neighbour as we love ourselves? If we treated others as we ourselves would like to be treated? If we took the trouble to pause and imagine how the other person feels about the way we are behaving towards them sexually? I think it means that we would not get our sexual kicks at another person's expense. We would not have sex unless the other person wanted it. We would not use our turn-ons to make another person feel humiliated or ashamed. We would use them to make people feel good about themselves and we would take the trouble to check out that that's what's happening. At very least, loving our neighbour as we love ourselves means recognizing that if the sex is not working for both people then it isn't working – period.

If we accept that, and I think we have to if we take Christ's commandment on board, then one factor becomes more important than any other in assessing the rights or wrongs of sexual behaviour: consent. Consent is the sine qua non of ethical sex. It is not always a sufficient condition – a woman might consent to sex with someone even though she is in a committed monogamous relationship with somebody else – but it is a necessary one. In an area as complex as sexuality I am wary of absolutes, but I really do believe there are no exceptions to that rule.

Hopefully this sounds obvious. Sadly, mainstream heterosexual society has yet to take it on board. When Jim Hodkinson was sacked as chief executive of the clothes chain New Look in the year 2000 for patting a woman employee on the bottom at an office party, there was a great deal of controversy about flirting at work and political correctness gone mad, but the word 'consent' was never used in any of the discussions I came across. 'There's nothing wrong with patting women's botties,' was what one TV show punter said without any reference to whether the woman wanted to have her 'botty' patted or not. But the fact is that if a woman does not want to have her bum patted, then it shouldn't happen. The issue then is not about the rights or wrongs of bum-patting per se, but about consent and how you ascertain it when you are approaching someone from behind, when you're the chief executive and she's an employee and when you don't know the woman in that kind of way.

The reason we are slow in getting to grips with this idea is that historically our understanding of consent has been crude – and that's putting it kindly. In 1678, Sir Matthew Hale declared it was impossible for a man to be charged with raping his wife because 'by their mutual matrimonial consent and contract the wife has given up herself in this kind unto her husband, which she cannot retract' (cited by McColgan in *Taking the Date Out of Rape*, p. 16). That's an understanding of consent that has been so twisted by men for the gratification of men it has become meaningless. As I said in chapter six, that law did not change until 1991 and even then it was controversial. In the early 1990s there was a spate of court cases which hinged on the concept of consent and thereby exposed the muddle of our thinking. In 1993 Austen Donnellan was found not guilty of rape after he had sex with a woman after a party. She said she had been very drunk and had crashed into bed to be woken by Donnellan's penis inside her. In 1994 David Warren, a student, was cleared of the charge of raping an 18-year-old woman. Her claim was that he had climbed on top of her and didn't stop when she told him to. In the same year, 21-year-old Ben Emerson was acquitted of rape. Even though the woman had told him she did not want to have intercourse, he had penetrated her when she had fallen asleep with her back to him. In each of these cases there is an issue about evidence. They all come down to her word against his and it is very difficult to convict on that basis. I am therefore not commenting on the verdicts. I am, however, commenting on the discussion that such cases evoked.

This is what the *Daily Mail* said in connection with the Donnellan and Warren cases and another incident in which an Oxford undergraduate was kicked out of Exeter College accused of sexually harassing a woman when they went for a walk along the river after a party:

Few girls are not warned by their parents or friends

about the sexual appetites of men. We were told the onus was on us to behave, and not 'to lead them on'. In short, we were told we should take responsibility for our own behaviour, as much as for the boys. And I still believe that to be true, old-fashioned and politically incorrect as it may sound. You do not lead a man on, unless of course you want what will probably, inevitably, follow . . . Lonely night walks along the river, sharing a bed or getting drunk and inviting him to your room in the early hours can be justifiably interpreted as not very discreet ways of inviting him to have sex with you. More importantly, there are few girls who are not aware of this. (*Daily Mail*, 17 October 1995)

I think this summation is spot on. Women have indeed been expected to take responsibility for men's sexualities as well as for their own. And it does depict the way in which we have traditionally thought about consent. We have been brought up to believe that if a woman shares a bed with a man or invites him back for a coffee or agrees to go for a walk along the river at night she is, in effect, consenting to vaginal intercourse.

It is no coincidence that lesbians, gay men and people who are into SM tend to be much better at thinking about consent than mainstream heterosexual society. The reason heterosexuals get confused is that traditionally thinking about sex has been orientated around sexual acts with the rightness or wrongness of those acts being assessed according to what men have defined as natural. In conventional sexual ethics it has been maintained that it is natural for a man to put his penis into a woman's vagina and he therefore can't be held responsible when he tries. It's therefore up to the woman to make sure she doesn't give him the opportunity. That's why you can't blame a man for trying to penetrate a woman when she's asleep – after all, it's only natural. This has been the framework of the sexual ethics we have inherited and while we recognize that consent must have a place in there, the controversy that surrounds so called 'date rape' suggests we haven't worked out what that place is. Lesbians, gay men and people into SM are in a position to cut through all that because they abandoned notions of 'natural' long ago. They therefore have a clean slate from which to think about consent.

This is how a friend describes going to cruising grounds with a view to having sex with a stranger:

> It's been my experience that there is very real kindness – I could almost use the word fellowship – amongst the men. Of course there are some selfish and sexually predatory characters about, but generally there is great kindness in the way the men treat each other, in the smile and in the wink. There's no compulsion. People are always free to pull out at the start or in the middle of sex. You are free to say: 'Sorry this isn't working for me,' and stop. I've done that often and it's happened to me often too. It seems so much more warm and honest than the kind of games heterosexuals play with all the scheming, chatting up and role play that goes on with the other sex.

There is no suggestion here that if a man has gone out cruising then he's obviously asking for it so he can't complain if a chap leaps on top of him and forces him into anal sex. Likewise when a lesbian asks another dyke back to her house for a coffee, she might hope sex is on the agenda but she has no trouble understanding that she does not have a right to it. And when a gay man sees a guy with a great arse wearing a pair of skin-tight jeans, its generally understood that that is no excuse to rape him. And when a woman is sucking the breasts of her lover and her lover says, 'Ow. That's hurting', the woman doesn't think she's entitled to carry on just because they're in bed together.

The most sophisticated thinking on consent I have come across is that of Guy Baldwin, a former International Mr Leather and psychotherapist whose clients include people who are into SM and fetish play. He says: 'Consent is a moment-by-moment gift' (Baldwin, *Ties that Bind*, p. 187). Contrast that with the idea that a woman consents for the rest of her life on the day she gets married. Baldwin says consent is like a traffic light in our heads which is showing either green, yellow or red. He says the traffic light works by testing actions with questions like – is it safe, does this feel good, is this what I want to be happening, is this what I need, is this what he needs, will I respect myself/him in the morning? He says that in order to have satisfaction from sex a person must be able to consult this inner traffic light and be able to respond to its information appropriately. When the light goes yellow or red, consent has been suspended and we have to find out why if we want the light to go green again. And that is the basis not just of ethical sex but of good sex too. Who wants the kind of sex where one person is getting his rocks off and the other is hurt, grudging, frightened or staring at the ceiling?

So, just in case there is anybody who is still confused

about consent, let me make it quite clear. Consenting to a walk down a river at night is not consenting to having your breasts fondled. Consenting to a kiss and a cuddle is not consenting to taking all your clothes off. Consenting to having sex with a lot of different men is not consenting to having sex with any and every man. Consenting to anal intercourse with a condom is not consenting to anal intercourse without a condom. Consenting to sleeping in the same bed is not consenting to vaginal intercourse. Consenting to sex on a Saturday night is not consenting to sex on Sunday morning. 'Consent is a moment-by-moment gift.'

There are times when people 'lead each other on' and very ugly it is too. It's commonplace and it's unkind. Women do it to men, women do it to women, men do it to men and men do it to women. A woman flirts outrageously with a man. He plucks up courage to ask her out and she turns him down gaining the satisfaction that he fancies her while he goes away with a blow to his ego. A man corners a single woman at a party and chats her up for the whole evening. She rides on the hope that her Bridget Jones' days are numbered while he conveniently omits to tell her he is married. Whenever this happens it boils down the same thing – vanity – and if we truly loved ourselves we wouldn't even feel tempted to do it. There is an art to making someone feel happy about themselves sexually while making it clear that this bit of flirting is as far as it goes. It is an art well worth cultivating. It is also worth cultivating the self-awareness to know when we are using our sexualities to make another person feel good and when we are massaging our own egos at another's expense.

And there are times when we make mistakes. Sometimes we genuinely misread people's signals. It's embarrassing, humiliating and disappointing when we imagine somebody wants to have sex with us when they don't. Or when we touch someone in a way we believe they will enjoy, and only find once we have done it that it made him or her feel uncomfortable. But if the mistake was genuine then the words 'I'm very sorry' shouldn't be too difficult to find. And when we do have to refuse someone's sexual advances or tell them that what they are doing does not turn us on, loving our neighbour as we love ourselves means taking care we do it in such a way as to minimize that person's sense of rejection. There are many ways of saying 'No' and some are a great deal kinder than others. 'Whatever you do, please remember to be kind to each other when you talk about sex together,' says Baldwin. 'We are all pretty sensitive about these things you know' (*Ties that Bind*, p. 157).

If we accept that consent is the key to good sex then there is a skill we need to develop to support that. We have to learn how to communicate. We must be prepared to speak. Talking about sex is important anyway if a couple wants to develop their sex life rather than let it plateau. It is not good enough for a woman to moan to her mates that her lover doesn't know how to give her an orgasm if she is not prepared to explain it to him. And it is recklessly irresponsible for a couple to have intercourse for the first time without exchanging words about it before they do. Quite apart from establishing consent, a couple need to reach an agreement about safety. A friend of mine, who is fitted with a coil, told a man who did not want to use a condom when they had vaginal intercourse that he needed to know she would never countenance having an abortion. These things are too important to be left unsaid. Most of the communication we do around sex is non-verbal – the catching of the eye, the touching of the knee, the pushing of the hands up under the shirt. That's what makes sex sex. But if we take consent seriously then there are times when our non-verbal communication has to be backed up with words. At the end of chapter five I gave the example of two men having unprotected anal intercourse. 'Are you sure?' asked one of them. 'Yes, I'm sure,' replied the other. They were few words but they were essential ones. Consent could not be assumed without them. Baldwin says that anyone who is unwilling to tolerate talking about sex cannot be presumed to be safe, sane and consensual (p. 156). The first question in cases of so-called date rape ought to be, 'What did you agree when you talked about intercourse?'

If we take consent seriously, if we place it right at the heart of our thinking about how we should treat each other, then we also need to attend to questions of the extent to which consent is genuine. Consent that is given under duress cannot properly be called consent at all. That means we need to pay attention to factors which might be inhibiting a person's capacity to say 'No'. If a woman is in a pub and a guy pats her bum and she doesn't like it, she can turn round and say, 'Can you not do that please?' It's harder for her to do that if it's the chief executive who does that at an office party. Rebuffing your boss has all sorts of other implications. That's one reason, and only one, why doctors, priests, therapists or chief executives need to be very careful about coming on to patients, parishioners, clients or employees. There is a risk that the person they are coming on to will 'consent' because they are confused, in awe or worried about what would happen if they didn't go along with it.

Once a friend of mine was talking, among much hollering and back-slapping with other men, about having sex with a prostitute. 'Tell me about the woman,' I said. 'Was she all right? What was going on for her?' He stared at me for a second. 'Of course she was all right, she was getting paid,' he said, and returned to the hollering and the general affirmation of his manliness. I go to church in Balsall Heath, an area that was once the notorious red light district of Birmingham. Through our church I know a group of women who befriend the women who work the streets. They tell me that there is a classic pattern to the way in which women get into prostitution. It generally starts with being sexually abused as children, an experience that erodes their sense of self and causes them to feel dislocated from their bodies. Then, when they are walking home from school, they get chatted up by pimps, who have developed an eye for a vulnerable young woman. The pimp gives the girl lots of attention and she calls him her boyfriend. He introduces her to drugs and then sends her out to work. By that time she is trapped because she is dependent. She has such little sense of self and so few positive experiences, she cannot imagine how her life could be other than it is. She is caught in a vicious circle – the more she feels alienated from her body, the more she depends on drugs, so the more money she needs, so the more she sells her body, so the more alienated from her body she feels.

'Of course the woman was all right,' said my friend, 'she was getting paid.'

I was once like my friend and maybe I still am in ways of which I am unaware. I used to be able to masturbate using top-shelf magazines without giving a moment's thought to the women who were in the photographs. That changed when I met the model Paula Hamilton, who told me how she came to be used in such magazines. Paula told me that when she was sixteen and desperate to be a model she signed on with a modelling agency and was offered a job in Spain for which she was to be paid £250 per week. She flew out full of excitement. When she got to the villa, the photographer's wife did her hair and make-up and wrapped a sarong round her telling her she was going to get the swimsuit. Paula went outside and the photographer who was setting up his equipment told her to drop her sarong. Paula protested that she hadn't got her swimsuit on. The photographer told her she could put it on later but for now, could she just drop the sarong and put her leg up? Much to Paula's relief the photographer's wife came out. Paula looked at her hands. There was no swimsuit. She started to cry. The photographer went to get a drink. His wife explained the shoot was to be nude photographs for Sweden and that every model started this way and that if she went home without doing the shoot she would owe them the airfare plus the fee. The pictures were subsequently published in *Penthouse* and *Mayfair*.

Michael Moorcock who has edited such magazines claims tricking women is standard practice in the pornography industry. He used to think soft porn was useful to society, believing it acted as a release for men's pent-up sexuality. After working at a porn publishers he changed his mind, partly because the letters to the magazines made it clear there was a connection between the material they published and violence against women, and partly because the women were being tricked.

> During photo-sessions, for instance, photographers were cajoling, 'egalitarian', friendly. After the sessions, however, they talked about the women in terms that were shockingly crude and brutal, joking about how they had tricked the 'girls' into lewd poses, sometimes by seducing them first. The 'girls', flattered, usually not very bright, frequently confused, were manipulated not just by the photographers into certain poses but also into signing release forms before they had seen the pictures. (Itzin (ed.), *Pornography*, pp. 541–2).

Now when I look at pictures of women in contrived poses with very few clothes on, I ask them: 'Who are you? What's your story? How did you come to be doing that?' I don't know the answers to those questions, but I believe those are the questions we ought to be asking if we agree it is never acceptable to get our sexual kicks at another person's expense. They certainly get in the way of settling down to a good wank.

When it comes to child pornography we already know the answers to those questions. We know the child has not consented because a child cannot consent to sex. In chapter four I explained Freud's theory that our sexualities are developing throughout our babyhoods and childhoods. It's not true to say that children aren't sexual. They are. Little boys have erections and little girls put soap up their vaginas when they are in the bath. The point is that when we are children our sexualities are very much in process. We do not have sufficient autonomy in our sexualities to be capable of consent. That is why sex with a child can never be right nor can taking photographs of children in ways designed to evoke a sexual response. Even possessing an image of that kind is to take part in child abuse. 'Interfere' is a good word to describe what happens when an adult touches a child for his or her sexual gratification. When an adult touches a child sexually, it gets right in there to the place of the child's becoming and interferes with the delicate and mysterious process through which he or she is developing. The adult walks away having had ten minutes of sexual thrill. The child experiences the disturbance of a process which can have consequences for the rest of his or her life.

Almost the whole of this chapter has been about consent. In stressing consent to the extent that I do, I am no doubt writing out of the experience of being a woman. For the most part it is women who have suffered as a result of our collective inability to get hold of what consent is all about. I have been groped, assaulted, followed, flashed at, wanked at, leered at and whistled at. I don't think that's anything exceptional. I think that's what it's like to be a young woman. Women's lives would be very different if every man at every bar and every builder on every building site understood that when a sexual encounter is not working for both people it is not working – period. Until they do, we need to emphasize consent.

But having said that, there is much more to loving our neighbours as we love ourselves than that. Consent is the minimum requirement of ethical sex. There are plenty more positive ways of loving our neighbours' sexualities as we love our own. Whenever we say to someone, 'You're looking really nice today,' we are doing something for them sexually. Whenever we decide not to have vaginal intercourse because of the risk of an unwanted pregnancy, we are taking care of a neighbour as yet unborn. Whenever we take the trouble to find out what really turns our partner on, we are loving our neighbour's sexuality. So are therapists who patiently attend to the sexual wounds of others. So are social workers when they assess if a child is at risk. So are the women who befriend the women who work the streets of Balsall Heath.

And so too are those who work to alleviate world poverty. So too are those who plant apple trees in inner cities. So too are those who teach us to swim. In chapter five I showed how sexuality is related to everything else about us. Being hungry, in pain or in distress affects our libidos. So does living in a grey built environment. So does being unfit because we haven't learnt to enjoy moving in water. Political campaigners, environmentalists and swimming teachers are not working primarily with sexuality, but happier sexuality can be a fruit of their labours nonetheless. Whatever we do to make the world a better place, it is likely that sexuality will be affected along the way. If we care about sexuality then we have got to get the National Health Service sorted out. Waiting 15 months for an operation affects people sexually, whatever that operation might be. If we care about sexuality then we need to cherish our children, attend to their questions and take them down to the park to play. Meeting the needs of children when they are children means they are less likely to grow into adults who over-burden sex with unmet needs. When a woman sets up a shop selling glamorous clothes for big women, she is taking care of sexuality. In helping women look good and feel proud of themselves she is contributing to their capacity to be turned on. Whenever we listen to others, whenever we raise their self-esteem, whenever we enable them to trust their bodies, we are loving our neighbours' sexualities as we love our own.

Right at the end of St John's Gospel there is a story in which the risen Christ has a meal with his disciple, Simon Peter:

> After the meal Jesus said to Simon Peter, 'Simon son of John, do you love me more than these others do?' He answered, 'Yes Lord, you know I love you'. Jesus said to him, 'Feed my lambs'. A second time he said to him, 'Simon son of John, do you love me?' He replied, 'Yes, Lord, you know I love you'. Jesus said to him, 'Look after my sheep'. Then he said to him a third time, 'Simon son of John, do you love me?' Peter was upset that he asked him the third time, 'Do you love me?' and said, 'Lord, you know everything; you know I love you'. Jesus said to him, 'Feed my sheep.' (John 21.15–17)

To love Christ is to feed his sheep. To love sexuality is to do exactly the same.

'Whatever you do,' said the former International Mr Leather, 'please remember to be kind.'

Chapter Nine

Love God

What does it mean to love God? In what way is loving God different from loving our neighbour and loving ourselves? What is this extra thing that Jesus is asking of us? And, while we're at it, who or what is God anyway? These are the questions with which this chapter is concerned. It is worth noting, however, that the previous two chapters were about God as well as this one. 'God is love,' says St John, 'and anyone who lives in love lives in God' (1 John 4.16). In learning how to love ourselves and love our neighbours we are living in God. That is why the commandment to love each other is *like* the commandment to love the Lord our God. Being confused about the difference between the two probably means we have got something right. And yet Jesus does ask something more of us than loving ourselves and loving each other. He says the most important commandment is that we love God with all our hearts, with all our souls and with all our minds. Sexuality, as we have already discovered, is intricately connected to our hearts, our souls and our minds. Jesus is telling us to love God with that part of our beings that moistens and yearns and swells. Whatever does he mean by that?

At this point, I am going to change gear and talk more personally about my own sexuality and how it is a part of my relationship with God. I do so because this is the most authoritative voice through which I can speak of the divine. That is not to say I discover God all on my own or that the communities and tradition to which I belong do not play an integral role in my knowing of God. Of course they do. When I am speaking of God, I am speaking of the God I have discovered through the practice of Christianity; its rituals, stories, songs, architecture and people. In saying what it means to love God, I am speaking out of my lived experience of faith. I offer it not because it is the definitive word on the matter but because it is my hope that through telling my own story I will enable other people to appreciate their own.

Most of my thinking about sexuality is based on my experience of being single. I don't quite know when you stop being a child and start being a single, but if we take the age at which I had my first boyfriend – 17 – as the beginning of my years of singledom, and the time I got married at the age of 37 as the end (for now), then I have been single for more than half my life. Doubtless this bias is reflected in this book and that is no bad thing – enabling people who are single to live their sexualities well is not something the Church has been good at in the past. My 20 years of being single were 20 years of the roving eye, 20 years of chatting up and of being chatted up, 20 years of no sex at all followed by the kind of intense sexual activity that often characterizes the start of a relationship, 20 years of scanning the personal ads, 20 years of introducing boyfriends to my other friends, 20 years of plucking up courage to call, 20 years of telling myself I was better off single, 20 years of surprising joys and bitter disappointments, 20 years of thinking that round any corner I might just meet someone who was going to change my life in a fundamental way.

Most of the time throughout those 20 years sex mattered an awful lot. I remember an older woman saying to me, 'Sex is important to you, isn't it?' At the time I didn't even understand the question. Of course sex was important to me. Wasn't it important to everybody? During those years I sometimes had a lover and sometimes didn't. When I didn't, I used to miss sex. I would be out driving, walking or swimming and experience a horniness that was sometimes a buzzy feeling and at other times more like an ache, a physical pain. There is a myth that the libido of men is more powerful than that of women. I don't believe it.

I was always looking for a sexual partner. The intensity and means through which I looked varied. During the times when I had a boyfriend, one part of me would be enjoying who he was for the present, while another part would be wondering if I ought to be finishing the relationship so that I could be open to finding someone to whom I was better suited. During the periods when I didn't have a partner, I would sometimes seize the day and go out on the pull, while at other times I would look by not looking on the grounds that I was more likely to find someone if I was content as I was. I looked when I went to a party. I looked when I went on retreat. I looked when I got on the bus.

During my years of being single there was an image of God that seemed in some way to reach into the part of my being from which my randiness came. It became most vivid for me when praying in a Benedictine monastery, something I describe in my first book:

The monastic church was modern, in fact it was still being built. From the outside it looked like a spaceship dropped into the countryside. On the approach all that could be seen was scaffolding, a windowless wall of bricks and an upturned saucer for a roof. Inside there was nothing; vast expanses of nothing between the mighty pyramid pillars, between the sloping ground and concrete circus-ring ceiling. There was nothing on the altar, nothing on the yellow brick walls, nothing on the floor but a dull, pile-less carpet. There was nothing to taste, nothing to smell, nothing to hear.

There was a thick, inviting silence. Distilled prayer was in the air.

I would sit literally for hours, leaning against the back, left-hand pillar, inwardly unpeeling in response to the nakedness of the building. Just being there felt like prayer. It was enough to sit or lie, absorbing the sense of the presence of God communicated in the stillness, in the space and in something else unknown.

The roof was a mighty wheel, its diameter almost the width of the entire building. Its huge circumference rested on the eight plain pillars spaced around the edge. The spokes of the wheel were myriad concrete arms reaching out to the limits, the rim, and connecting all that is to the paradox, the hub. There at the convergence was a concrete opening, glimpses of the sky, aperture of beyond.

I would be drawn to look at the roof at the point

at which the monks sang the beautiful song from Colossians:

He is the image of the invisible God,
the first-born of all creation;
for in him all things that were created,
in heaven and earth, visible and invisible.
All things were created through him and for him;
he is before all things, and in him all things hold
    together.

As I listened to these words and looked at this roof, feeling stripped in the bareness of the building, a very sexual picture of God emerged.

I saw God as huge. Big like the outer concrete ring, bigger than anything I could think of and therefore bigger than the Bible, bigger than religious meetings, bigger than the church. He was bigger than Christianity, bigger than the world. Through Jesus everything that was not Jesus himself (cups of coffee, tropical rain forests, Asian culture, logical positivism, dreadful jokes) had been made. In Jesus everything that there was in this world was held in arms like spokes containing all creation, pointing to its source, its centre, its light, beyond . . .

I saw that all of life had but one source, God, and what is more that source was in me. (*Fat is a Spiritual Issue*, pp. 68–70)

And when I prayed in this way in that church, I had another of those experiences for which my culture had not prepared me – I became sexually aroused.

Conceptualizing God as the energy that pulsates through the whole cosmos, included me, stirred me in a way that was deeper than any turn-on I had had before. I imagined the spokes of the wheel/roof as the myriad arms of Christ drawing the whole creation to himself. I saw them as the same arms that were 'opened wide for us on the cross', as it says in the eucharistic prayer. Christ's love was so immense that he opened wide his arms to hold the world together in one song – a uni-verse. I saw God as the being who is before all things, the spirit which infuses all things, the love which longs for all things and which will never let us go. God is sexy.

And that is how I understood erotic energy. I thought of that reaching out and holding of all things together as the erotic stuff of God; God extending, God reaching, God filling, God surrounding. So when I too was yearning and longing and reaching out I saw that as my taking part in God's erotic work. When I was able to see the connections between literary criticism, philosophy, theology and early psychology, as I was in Coleridge's *Biographia*, I understood that as my partaking in Christ's movement of holding together all things in unity. And when I found myself aching and craving for someone I couldn't have, I saw that as the calling of God in my libido, gathering into consciousness the unlived parts of myself, bringing to life the dormant aspects of my personhood. And when I met a stranger in a pub and met his eye and met his mind and brought him home, I saw that as me reaching out and drawing him in just as Christ is drawing all creation to the groin of his being.

At the time that I was writing *Fat is a Spiritual Issue* I used to imagine I was the only person who had ever conceptualized God and sex in this way. It was only once it had been published and I started to read up on sexuality that I discovered a body of writing that intimates something very similar. I was very excited to discover that the concept of eros, the Greek word for love from which our words erotic and erogenous are derived, is all about the kind of yearning and longing and holding all things together in unity that I found so resonant. As far back as the sixth century, a mystical theologian called Pseudo-Dionysius described eros as the divine longing:

> And we may be so bold as to claim . . . that the Cause of all things loves all things in the superabundance of his goodness, that because of this goodness he makes all things, brings all things to perfection, holds all things together, returns all things. The divine longing (eros) is Good seeking good for the sake of Good. (Pseudo-Dionysius, *The Divine Names*, 4.10, cited in Sheldrake, *Befriending our Desires*, p. 26)

The American psychologist Rollo May describes eros as 'the drive towards union with what we belong to' (cited in Sheldrake, p. 58). The hermit monk William McNamara says: 'I mean erotic in the radical sense of that word, in its real meaning: a reaching and stretching with every fiber of one's body-person for the fullness of life' (*Mystical Passion*, p. 8). Ann Ulanov defines eros as 'the psychic urge to relate, to join, to be in-the-midst-of, to reach out to, to value, to get in touch with, to get involved with concrete feelings, things and people, rather than to abstract or theorize' (*The Feminine*, p. 155).

And so, throughout my years of being single, that was

the image of God and of sexuality that endured. It was a vision of sexuality that resonated with my sense of sex more profoundly than the much more common conceptualization of it as the attraction between male and female. I found the male/female distinction too flat, too polarized and too dualistic to describe the things that turned me on. It left little space for God as an integral aspect of sexuality. What made much more sense to me was to see the primary sexual energy as that of Christ who is holding all creation together. I thought of the attraction between male and female as part of that erotic yearning, even the dominant motif for many of us, but I saw the erotic tug as coming from a deeper source than that. It was also about the longing for connection, the need for belonging, the desire to be centred in the source of the universe. 'Deep is calling to deep' is how the Psalmist describes prayer (Psalm 43.7). It was indeed and I could feel it in my groin.

When Jesus tells us to love the Lord our God with all our hearts, with all our souls and with our minds, I believe he is asking us to love God with our sexualities. He is inviting us to attend to our turn-ons, to listen to their intimations, to dare to believe that God is the source of them. I do not believe we are turned on by flesh alone but by every word that come from the mouth of God. Whenever we are aroused, whether that be through the curve of a breast, the touch of a hand or the word understood, it is God who is luring us, wooing us and drawing us on. To be sexual is to take part in God's desiring for the whole creation. To love God with our sexualities is to adore God because of that – with everything we have.

And yet that is not the whole story. In fact the point of the next part of my account of sexuality and my relationship with God is that we never do get hold of the whole story, nor should we try. When I reached the age of 33, something was to happen that was to have a profound impact on my sexuality. I woke up one morning with a strange pins-and-needles sensation in my feet that I thought must be to do with the way in which I had been sleeping. I began to doubt that, when it hadn't gone away three days later and had spread all the way up my legs. I noticed I was feeling permanently exhausted and was having to concentrate coming down the stairs because I had lost the sense of where my feet were in space. Gradually, moving my legs became as difficult as moving rods of iron. When I began to lose my vision too I was diagnosed with multiple sclerosis.

To say it was a shock was an understatement. I must have been in a state of shock for about nine months. I went from being a fit, healthy woman living in community, earning my living as a journalist, writing books, giving seminars, singing and playing the piano, swimming three times a week, having boyfriends and using my holidays to travel the world, to someone who struggled to walk and felt a weariness that a good night's sleep could barely touch. I changed from someone who would travel down to London from Birmingham just for the evening, to someone for whom the effort of getting up the road to post a letter seemed overwhelming. I changed from someone who imagined life in all its fullness stretched out before her, to someone who wondered how long she had got before she was blind and using a wheelchair.

And during that period of my illness my libido totally disappeared. I can't remember well enough to put an exact time on it, but for at least a year I didn't experience the slightest bit of moistening in my groin. I was numb physically and metaphorically from the waist down. Sexual fantasies that could once have been depended upon to get me going completely lost their potency. I would try to recall my sexiest sex in an attempt to rekindle some horny feelings. There was nothing there. By that time I had already written the line, 'I felt randy for the whole of Birmingham' (p. 7), but the person who had written that seemed like an alien.

All of this is totally understandable. There were many different explanations for my loss of libido. Most people know what it is like to feel too tired for sex. The fatigue that comes with multiple sclerosis was in a different league from a tired-at-the-end-of-a-hard-week kind of weariness. I had to conserve what energy I had for doing things like going to the toilet and getting something to eat. I had nothing spare for the puffing and panting of orgasm. And I had lost sensation from the waist down. When I crapped it felt like little needles pricking the inside of my anus. It was just the same with my vagina and legs. Those feelings weren't particularly uncomfortable in themselves. What was uncomfortable was being reminded I had an incurable degenerative disease.

And I was undergoing an identity crisis. 'Who am I?' was a question I was asking at every level. 'You're still the same Jo,' my friends would say, but I didn't feel like the person I once knew. I used to think of myself as a sharp mind in a curvy body. I began to rethink myself in terms of orange stickers and access for the disabled.

Today I have no problem claiming 'disabled' as part of my identity. I recognize that everybody is disabled to some extent and if they aren't at this moment, they will be one day. Sometimes I can walk easily and other times I can't, and I slip in and out of a disabled identity accordingly. I am happy about this now, but I had to do a bit of work to get there.

On top of all that, I was terrified. I have always said that fear is the most debilitating symptom of multiple sclerosis. It is possible, actually, to lead a full and happy life without being able to see. It isn't possible to lead a full and happy life when every emotion is choked by a sense of dread. I knew this but I didn't know how not to be afraid. I would go to bed yearning for the oblivion of sleep but once there I was too afraid to let go into unconsciousness. When I did sleep, often as a result of being knocked out by alcohol, the first thing I would do on waking was check my limbs to see if any more had abandoned me during the night. Some people are turned on through fear but I'm not one of them. When I'm afraid I freeze. 'Frigid' is an unkind word, but it does have the right root to it. So when I say I lost my libido through having multiple sclerosis, that was not just one reason to go off sex, it was five. And if five reasons weren't enough, it corresponded to a period in my life when I was having some careless sexual counselling which was quite enough to put anyone off sex for a long, long time.

So what did this experience tell me about sexuality and God? What did it mean to love God with my sexuality when I wasn't feeling sexual any more? Some might say we should look to the healthy rather than the sick to reveal the nature of sexuality to us, but that would be to take a very low view of illness. I would go so far as to say one reason we become ill is to discover the truths we miss in the energy, optimism and illusion of independence that being well brings. I don't think it's a coincidence that at a time when I was reading, talking and writing about sexuality, I developed a disease that caused my own to go AWOL.

At this time of my life it was astonishing to recognize how something that I had thought of as such an essential part of my personhood – my libido – could just disappear. Given all that I have said about the connection between sexuality and God in the previous pages, we might deduce that if I had lost my libido, I had lost my sense of the presence of God too. And yet nothing could have been further from the truth. As I slowly began to come to terms with my illness, as I falteringly adapted to my changed and changing body, I discovered a new way of being, a different dimension of the divine.

At the start of my illness, I found thoughts of the future very difficult to deal with. My body had become strange and unpredictable. I didn't know from one day to the next what I was going to be capable of. I had to come to terms with a prognosis which ranged from 'you might get better and never have another episode again', to 'you might be blind, unable to walk and incontinent within the next few years'. Well-meaning friends who attempted to give me hope by suggesting I might be one of the lucky ones who had the disease mildly brought no solace at all. I needed to take hold of the truth of our existence – and that is the truth for all of us, not just people with MS – which is that we are not in control. We do not know what the morning brings, nor who we will become. My response to this awareness was to claim the present moment for what it is and attempt to do nothing more than live in it: I do not know what tomorrow holds, but I know this moment is a good moment in which to be alive. Buddhism, as I understand it, is particularly good at enabling us to practise this. The Buddhist monk Thich Nhat Hanh suggests a form of meditation in which we learn to live in the present moment through becoming conscious of our breath:

> Breathing in, I calm my body.
> Breathing out, I smile.
> Dwelling in the present moment,
> I know this is a wonderful moment!

(*Present Moment, Wonderful Moment*, p. 32)

A lot of the time it was a struggle. There were plenty of times when my meditation was just a meditation on how frightened I was rather than a focus on my breathing. But there were other times when I would reach a moment of stillness in which I realized that this moment does indeed hold everything I need. The God of my yearning became the God who is enough. I cannot describe this any better than Kat Duff in her book *The Alchemy of Illness*, which is about her experience of chronic fatigue and immune dysfunction syndrome, or ME, as it is more commonly known in Britain:

> When I'm well, I tend to fill my days with a multitude of meaningful activities – my counselling practice, my

writing, a lover, friends and godchildren, political involvements and spiritual practices; but when I get sick, even with minor ailments, I lose my motivation. After six months with CFIDS, I could not remember why I had ever wanted to hike those trails, teach those classes, or attend those meetings. Nothing seemed worth doing – and that awareness shimmered with power. I remember the exact time and place I first realized its enormity; I was sitting on the living-room couch after a long, tiring morning of work, holding a small bowl of rice in my hands. The phone rang, and – quite out of character – I just sat there and let it ring, as I turned the bowl in my hands and admired its perfect shape. I felt privy to one of the world's great secrets: that what *is* is enough, that each moment contains, like the circle of that bowl, the whole of creation in the space it offers, and we need not go anywhere or do anything to find it. Since then there have been times when I have cried bitterly over the losses wrought by my illness, but more often than not I have cherished the serenity of being still and feeling full with the moment at hand, of not wanting anything more than I already have. (*The Alchemy of Illness*, p. 43)

And so I embraced a new way of living. It was slow. It was simple and it was very, very intimate. 'Let all mortal flesh keep silence' is how an ancient liturgical hymn begins (*English Hymnal*, 318). The angels had said to my libido 'Ssssssssh!' and I discovered the God who is as near to us as breath.

The commandment to love God with all our hearts,

with all our souls and with all our minds, is, I believe, a commandment never to make anything, no matter how good, more important than God. To make an idol of something is to put something in the place of God, to locate it in the centre of our lives where it doesn't quite belong. It is very tempting to make an idol out of sex, especially as sex can, at its best, bring us the nearest many of us get to heaven in this lifetime. And I think that is precisely what we, as a society, do. We place an enormous premium on being sexy. Attractive people, whatever we might mean by that, are valued over those considered unattractive. Having sex three times a week is believed to be good for your health, much like taking vitamins and drinking plenty of water. The psycho-analyst Susie Orbach says that as a society we see the erotic as a central part of our lives. 'People are under tremendous pressure to have fulfilling physical relation-ships,' she says 'and when they don't they feel a sense of shame and keep it secret' (*Daily Mail*, 28 November 2002).

I think that if we burden our sexualities with such an intolerable weight of expectation then sooner or later we are going to come unstuck. Sex is not like food, some-thing we cannot survive without. It is more puckish, more mysterious, more will-o'-the-wisp than that. Our libidos disappear, they change shape, they vary in inten-sity. We can no more say what they are than we can define the shape of an amoeba. Sometimes we experience being turned on as a central and essential part of our beings. Other times it seems at the periphery and as irrelevant as caviar. Sometimes we want sex like we want to stay alive. Other times we want it like we want a cup of tea. Sometimes an orgasm is like scratching an insect bite. Other times it's like being rent open and exploding through the cosmos. Jeffrey Weeks talks about the 'plasticity' of sex (*Sexuality and its Discontents*, p. 122). I think that is a very good description. We will be disappointed and distorted if we try to cling onto it. To live sex well is to learn to hold it lightly.

To love God with all our hearts and souls and minds is to resist making a god out of sexuality. It is one thing to see our sexualities as part of our way towards God. It is another thing to be ashamed because we are not feeling horny. It is one thing to thoroughly enjoy being turned on. It is another to invest our identity in our capacity to moisten and yearn and swell. It is one thing to recognize that sex can make us more deep, loving and sensuous as people. It is another thing to say we can't achieve the same results through celibacy – monks and nuns do a great service in giving the lie to that myth. There will always be periods in our lives when, for whatever reason, be that illness or contentment, childhood or old age, menopause or pregnancy, winter cold or summer heat, our sexualities fade to the back consciousness and we get on with feeding the baby or undergoing chemotherapy or doing whatever it is that needs to be done. To love God is to cherish those times as much as our times of being turned on. It is to go with the flow of our sexualities rather than to contrive ourselves into horniness when horny is what we are not. It is to use *all* of our hearts and *all* of our souls and *all* of our minds as a way of knowing God and not get stuck in one particular form of relating. To love God is to know that God is both utterly in our sexualities and utterly other than them too.

It is to embrace our sexualities, to say 'yes' to them, to dare to plunge in and discover God through them. It is also to love the God of silence, the God of breath, the God who is enough.

Today, as I sit and type, I have the full use of my limbs. In fact I have had only one episode of multiple sclerosis in the past 18 months. In an illness which is as capricious as MS, I am loathe to make predictions, but it seems that I am indeed one of those in whom the disease has progressed slowly. I even dare to hope that my scars might be healing. But the disease affects my life on a daily basis nonetheless. I have less energy than my peers. I have to be constantly vigilant, taking care not to put my body into situations of unnecessary stress. I am able to travel to London, for example, but I have to build in rest time around it to recover. Every so often I experience what I call 'waterfall legs' which is a pins-and-needles sensation cascading down my thighs and into my feet. I know from experience that that is the beginning of an MS episode, and sometimes, if I respond quickly and effectively enough, I can stop that becoming a full-blown attack: I tell my boss I am working from home, I cancel everything in my diary, I lie low and give my body everything it needs.

As for my libido, it has returned but with nothing like the rampant energy that I had before I was ill. I now have what I would call a workable sexuality. When I was in my twenties my first orgasm was just the beginning of sex, an aperitif. Today one orgasm is all I have an appetite for. It is possible that my sexuality has changed for other reasons too. I am more content today than I was when I was single. Maybe that contentment has quietened my libido. Perhaps it has been the other way round. Who knows? 'The wind blows wherever it pleases. You hear its sound, but you cannot tell where it comes from or where it is going,' said Jesus (John 3.8). He was talking about the Holy Spirit. It sounds like sexuality to me.

I have changed in other ways too. Living with multiple sclerosis has made me very aware that we are not in control, that at any moment we could lose our legs, our hands, our heart. By the same token any one of us, however holy, could become mentally ill. I have a disease which affects my central nervous system, but I could have had a disease which affected my brain. I had known what it was like to lose my legs but I might have been discovering what it was like to lose my mind. When my fatigue was at its worst and I lay in bed looking at the cards, presents and flowers that surrounded me, I felt very aware that nothing could be worse than being unloved. But what if I had an illness that had made me difficult to love? At the time I lived next door to a care-in-the-community home from which a resident had attempted to smash our front door down with a brick. I could have had an illness that had caused me to behave in that kind of way. Would people have loved me as much if I had? I doubt it.

While I was meditating on this, spending hour after hour in my bed thinking about the contingency of our existence, one truth became important above all others and that is the truth that whoever we are and whatever we become, we are loved by God. Even the love of my friends, solid and humbling as it was, would be challenged if I was to become antisocial through changes to my mind. The confidence I discovered I could take with me through all my unknown becomings was the truth that I was loved by God. I could not say who I was going to become, but whoever that was and whatever I was to be, I was going to be loved by the one who had made me. Taking hold of that truth and allowing it to permeate throughout my being caused me to re-evaluate my thinking about marriage.

When I was younger, I was very angry about marriage, and, in all honesty, still am. As an institution marriage has a pretty grubby history. Until the middle of the nineteenth century it was analogous to the slave trade in that it involved women losing their names, their legal identities and their rights to their own bodies. It has changed since then. It is no longer the case that women have the same legal identity as their husbands or that they have a duty to have sex whenever the man wants it, though it took until 1991 for that to be acknowledged in law (see p. 89). Nonetheless, I had found it very difficult to take part in an institution which for so many centuries has been the linchpin of the very patriarchy that everything in me railed against. Nothing is beyond redemption and even marriage can, I believe, evolve into a system that benefits women. The big question for me has been whether it is worth redefining or whether it is best, as Germaine Greer advised, to refuse to tie the knot (*The Female Eunuch*, p. 358).

My experience of having multiple sclerosis has helped me to find a way of thinking about marriage that I could live with integrity. If I believe, as I do, that God loves us as we are, as we have been and as we shall be, then I also believe that we are called to love and to be loved by each other in the same way. It is not good enough to say that God loves us in one way, but we do something completely different. If God loves us through all our different becomings, then we are to learn what it means to love like that too. There are many different ways in which we can live that calling out. Parents can get a good handle on what loving unconditionally means. So can those who live in community. So can those who care for the mentally ill. Marriage, as I understand it, is one more way of doing that. It is a commitment to grow in the knowledge of God's love through the discipline of loving one particular person whoever he or she might become. Those who lament that their partner is not the person they married have, by my way of thinking, missed the point. The point is to learn to love and be loved as God loves us, which is a love which endures through failure, through depression, through Alzheimer's, through AIDS, through loss of faith, through loss of hair, through loss of limb.

And so it was that I decided to get married. Well it wasn't quite as simple as that actually. It was a coming together of those thought processes with the circumstances in which I found myself, but I don't want to say too much about that. It is one thing to tell my story. It is another to tell somebody else's. This makes writing about marriage something of a dilemma. In saying 'I decided to get married', I don't mean, either, that I swallowed wholesale the Church's teaching on the subject. I still question some of the rituals of church ceremonies, the notion of marriage as 'given' and the idea that it can only take place between a man and a woman. I believe that marriage needs to be reinterpreted in every age, including this one. The difference is that I am now contributing to that reinterpretation from the inside. Before, I challenged it from without. Another difficulty in writing about marriage is that it is a way of life I am only just beginning. As I sit and type, I have been married for a year so my understanding of it, and of the God I discover through it, are not as well developed as my understanding of being single. I am writing from the steep point of the learning curve.

What I can do, however, is talk about the immediate difference that marriage made to me, and immediate the difference certainly was. From the time I woke up on the morning after our wedding, I felt as though my inner world was being rearranged. The difference was in being held. I was held before I was married, of course, but I experienced it differently the other side of the dotted line. Before I had said those words and signed that document there was always the option of finishing the relationship. I even considered that on the morning of the wedding. In marrying I closed that option off for good. Before I married I was holding my partner for now, for as long as it seemed like the right thing to do. After I was married I was holding him for ever; the baby and child he once was, the person he is today, the old man that, hopefully, he will become. The more I knew that was how I was holding him, the more I knew that was how I was being held in return.

And that commitment seemed to move us into another realm; a bigger, more expansive place. I felt like a child in a newly changed bed who couldn't reach to the bottom of the crisp, clean sheets no matter how far she stretched. I felt as though I'd got a mother again. I felt like playing. It was fun. I felt like sleeping too. Our commitment was a pillow into which I could lay my head after all those years of yearning. 'Enough for me to keep my soul tranquil and quiet, like a child in its mother's arms, as content as a child that has been weaned,' says the Psalmist (Psalm 131.2). I felt like a baby that had finished her sucking and was going to sleep at the breast with her mouth still open.

But that wasn't all that was going on. Marriage was working on different levels at the same time. God had become my glow. It was not just the love between my partner and myself that was expanding, it was also God that I was loving with all my heart, with all my soul and with all my mind. The love that we were playing in was God's love for us. The delight that we experienced was God's delight in us. The hope that we would love each other whoever we became was a mere slither of the bigger truth of God's enduring love for us. I very much want to grow old with my lover, but even if he dies before that happens, I believe that through our marriage, however brief it might have been, I am better able to grasp the breadth and the length, the height and the depth, the playful and the pillow-esque love of God:

> Where can I go to escape your spirit?
> Where can I flee from your presence?
> If I climb the heavens, you are there.
> There too, if I lie in Sheol.
> If I flew to the point of sunrise,
> Or westward across the sea,
> Your hand would still be guiding me.
> Your right hand holding me. (Psalm 139.7–10)

And all of this has affected me sexually. This sense of being held, this practice of the God who will never let us go, has changed my experience of sex. In the past, sex was something that connected me to other people. It was a way of reaching out, a way of drawing other people into intimacy. Now that I am married, sex is not so much a way of drawing people in but a line that keeps them out. It is a boundary that defines my relationship with my partner against all my other relationships. At first I found that experience of sex difficult to reconcile with the image of God drawing all creation together that I had found so potent in the past. Increasingly, however, I have found myself returning to that picture of God from the book of Colossians. It is as though I am exploring a different dimension of it, the dimension of time rather than space. When I was single it was the arms of Christ connecting all people and all things that resonated with my ubiquitous sexuality. Now, it is the arms of Christ holding us throughout all our becomings which makes sense of my sexual experience. When we married, I included these sentences in the wedding service: 'Before the world began – you are loved. When the old order passes away and the new creation comes – you are loved.' I wrote those words not because I fully understood them but because they seemed to articulate the mystery we were committed to explore, namely that we are held by God from that place at which time ceases to exist. Making a lifelong commitment to my partner is an intimation of the timeless love of God. Sex has become a way of exploring that mystery, a reaching out across a lifespan rather than across a crowded pub.

In some respects, however, sex is more stressful than it

was before. At the time of writing I am 38. I would love to make a baby with this man who is capable of communicating these truths of God to me, and I feel we haven't much time left. This in itself is bringing a whole new dimension to my experience of sex, namely an agenda. For the 20 years I was single I had sex without having intercourse. A side-effect of that choice was that sex was playful with no goal other than that of giving each other pleasure, if 'pleasure' isn't too simple a word for it. Now I want a baby, sex is about more than pleasure and it does have a goal. Like many in this situation, I am discovering that it is all too easy to become so focused on making a baby that we forget to make love in the process. There is a tension between my belief that we should only have sex when both of us want to and the need to get randy because the urine stick says I'm ovulating.

This is another situation in which the commandment to love God with all my heart, with all my soul and with all my mind is very useful. It causes me to recognize the truth that nothing is more important than God, not even something as awesome as becoming a mother. It is all too easy for baby-wanting couples to get into a downward spiral in which the more wound-up they become about conception, the more difficult sex becomes and so the more wound-up they become about conception. A way out of that all-too-familiar spiral is to be able to hold sex and its outcomes more lightly through the recognition that God is the source of our joy, God alone is the giver of life and we will live in love, creativity and gratitude whether we have a baby or not.

Jesus tells us that the most important commandment is

to love the Lord our God with all our heart, with all our soul and with all our mind. I do not claim to have done anything more than begun to find out what that means but I believe it includes loving our neighbour as we love ourselves and it means more than that as well. It means relishing our capacity to turn on and to be turned on, but at the same time not identifying with that part of ourselves to such an extent that when we lose it we wonder who we are or where God has gone. It means never making anything more important than God to us, not even something as delicious as sex or as womb-tugging as making a baby. It means being wooed by God, being seduced by God, opening to the lover God, the lover who bears gifts, gifts that are always new.

Epilogue
What Is Sexuality?

I began this book by asking, 'What is sexuality?' I finish it feeling like a farmer in a Chinese landscape painting – very, very small beside the awesome mountain of my subject matter. I never answered that question fully. I don't believe that anybody ever will. The more we try to grasp sexuality, the more it expands out of our reach. Sexuality can point us to God or it can lead us to an inner hell. It can be an all-compassing force or it can disappear altogether. It is both enduring and ephemeral, earthy and mystical, universal and peculiarly our own. We can study sex for years, enjoy it for a lifetime, think about it right to the edges of our brains, but we never really take hold of it. We do not grasp. We glimpse.

But as we enter into the mystery of sexuality, as we engage with it, despair of it and attend to its glorious intimations, we can discover something of what it would mean to live our sexualities well. What would it mean to love myself with the part of my being that moistens and yearns and swells? What would it mean to love my neighbour? What would it mean to love the Lord our God? These are the questions that we can put in our handbags, bring with us to prayer or work out with a partner as we play between the sheets. Whoever we are, whether a woman about to undergo a hysterectomy, a man about to go out cruising, a couple trying for a baby, a woman who loves another woman, or a teenager making her way through the eyes that beckon and the hands that grope, we can use our sexualities to let love grow.

I am not making out that the answers to those questions will always be easy. On the contrary, I believe that finding out what it means to love and be loved is a life-long journey. There will always be sexual dilemmas. There will be times when there will be a conflict between loving ourselves and loving our neighbour. There will be situations when loving one neighbour will be at variance with loving another. There will be moments, maybe even years, when we cannot work out who God is or what is going on. There will be periods when all we can do is live the questions in the hope that we will live along some distant day into the answer (Rilke, *Letters to a Young Poet*, p. 35). But I believe that wherever our dilemmas and whatever our sexualities might be, these are the right questions for us to be living. What does it mean to love myself? What does it mean to love my neighbour? What does it mean to love the Lord my God, here, where I am, with the sexuality that I have, right now?

What is sexuality?

Something which has existed from the beginning,
That we have heard,
And we have seen with our own eyes;
That we have watched
And touched with our hands ... (1 John 1.1)

Bibliography

Philosophy and language theory

Walter Truett Anderson (ed.), *The Fontana Post-Modernism Reader*, London: Fontana Press, 1996.

Richard Appignanes and Chris Garratt, *Postmodernism for Beginners*, Cambridge: Icon Books, 1995.

Roland Barthes, *The Pleasure of the Text*, Oxford: Blackwell, 1990.

Simon Blackburn, *Oxford Dictionary of Philosophy*, Oxford: Oxford University Press, 1996.

Alan Bullock *et al.* (eds), *The Fontana Dictionary of Modern Thought*, 2nd edn, London: Fontana Press, 1988.

Anthony Burgess, *A Mouthful of Air*, London: Vintage, 1992.

Paul Cobley and Litza Jansz, *Semiotics for Beginners*, Cambridge: Icon Books, 1997.

Samuel Taylor Coleridge, *Biographia Literaria*, London: J. M. Dent & Sons, 1975.

David Crystal, *Linguistics*, 2nd edn, London: Penguin Books, 1985.

David Crystal, *The Penguin Dictionary of Language*, 2nd edn, London: Penguin Books, 1999.

Jonathan Culler, *Saussure*, 2nd edn, London: Fontana Press, 1986.

Thomas Docherty (ed.), *Postmodernism: A Reader*, Hemel Hempstead: Harvester Wheatsheaf, 1993.

Robin Dunbar, *Grooming, Gossip and the Evolution of Language*, London: Faber and Faber, 1996.

Antony Flew (ed.), *A Dictionary of Philosophy*, London: Pan Books, 1979.

Terence Hawkes, *Structuralism and Semiotics*, London: Routledge, 1997.

John Heaton and Judy Groves, *Wittgenstein for Beginners*, Cambridge: Icon Books, 1994.

Richard Kearney and Mara Rainwater (eds), *The Continental Philosophy Reader*, London: Routledge, 1996.

David Lyon, *Postmodernity*, Buckingham: Open University Press, 1994.

John Lyons, *Introduction to Theoretical Linguistics*, Cambridge: Cambridge University Press, 1968.

Jane Mills, *Womanwords*, London: Virago, 1991.

Davis Pears, *Wittgenstein*, Glasgow: Fontana, 1971.

Steven Pinker, *The Language Instinct*, London: Penguin Books, 1994.

Richard Popkin and Avrum Stroll, *Philosophy Made Simple*, London: W. H. Allen, 1969.

Leland Ryken, *Triumphs of the Imagination: Literature in Christian Perspective*, Illinois: InterVarsity Press, 1979.

George Steiner, *Real Presences*, London: Faber and Faber, 1989.

Ludwig Wittgenstein, *On Certainty*, Oxford: Blackwell, 1975.

Ludwig Wittgenstein, *Tractatus Logico-Philosophicus*, London: Routledge & Kegan Paul, 1981.

T. R. Wright, *Theology and Literature*, Oxford: Blackwell, 1988.

Theology and spirituality

Rubem Alves, *The Poet, the Warrior, the Prophet*, London: SCM Press, 1990.

Paul Avis, *Eros and the Sacred*, London: SPCK, 1989.

Joanne Carlson Brown and Carole Bohm (eds), *Christianity, Patriachy and Abuse*, Cleveland: The Pilgrim Press, 1989.

Lavinia Byrne, *Women Before God*, London: SPCK, 1989.

Sheila Cassidy, *Good Friday People*, London: Darton, Longman & Todd, 1991.

Jim Cotter, *Pleasure, Pain and Passion: Some Perspectives on Sexuality and Spirituality*, 2nd edn, Sheffield: Cairns Publications, 1993.

Jim Cotter, *Prayer at Night: A Book for the Darkness*, 3rd edn, Exeter: J. E. Cotter, 1986.

David Ford, *Self and Salvation: Being Transformed*, Cambridge: Cambridge University Press, 1999.

Elaine Graham, *Making the Difference: Gender, Personhood and Theology*, London: Mowbray, 1995.

Thich Nhat Hahn, *Living Buddha, Living Christ*, London: Rider, 1996.

Thich Nhat Hahn, *Present Moment, Wonderful Moment*, London: Rider, 1993.

Rosemary Haughton, *The Passionate God*, London: Darton, Longman & Todd, 1981.

Margaret Hebblethwaite, *Motherhood and God*, London: Geoffrey Chapman, 1984.

Jo Ind, *Fat Is a Spiritual Issue: My Journey*, London: Mowbray, 1993.

Issues in Human Sexuality: A Statement by the House of Bishops of the General Synod of the Church of England, London: Church House Publishing, 1991.

Pope John Paul II, *Christian Family (Familiaris Consortio)* London: Catholic Truth Society, 1981.

Morton Kelsey and Barbara Kelsey, *Sacrament of Sexuality: The Spirituality and Psychology of Sex*, Shaftsbury: Element, 1991.

Carl Koch and Joyce Heil, *Created in God's Image: Meditating on Our Body*, Winona: Saint Mary's Press, 1991.

A. T. Mann and Jane Lyle, *Sacred Sexuality*, Shaftsbury: Element, 1995.

William McNamara, *Mystical Passion: The Art of Christian Living*, Shaftsbury: Element, 1991.

Gareth Moore, *The Body in Context: Sex and Catholicism*, London: SCM Press, 1992.

John Mumford, *Ecstasy through Tantra*, Minnesota: Llewellyn Publications, 1994.

James Nelson, *Embodiment: An Approach to Sexuality and Christian Theology*, Minneapolis: Augsburg Press, 1979.

James Nelson, *The Intimate Connection: Male Sexuality, Masculine Spirituality*, London: SPCK, 1992.

James Nelson and Sandra Longfellow (eds), *Sexuality and the Sacred: Sources for Theological Reflection*, London: Mowbray, 1994.

Pope Paul VI, *On Human Life (Humanae Vitae)*, London: Catholic Truth Society, 1999.

Pseudo-Dionysius, *The Complete Works*, New York: Paulist Press, 1987.

Philip Rawson, *The Art of Tantra*, London: Thames & Hudson, 1978.

Rosemary Radford Ruether, *Sexism and God-Talk*, London: SCM Press, 1983.

Letty Russell and J. Shannon Clarkson, *Dictionary of Feminist Theologies*, London: Mowbray, 1996.

Sangharakshita, *A Guide to the Buddhist Path*, Glasgow: Windhorse Publications, 1990.

Sangharakshita, *Buddhism for Today and Tomorrow*, Birmingham: Windhorse Publications, 1996.

Philip Sheldrake, *Befriending our Desires*, London: Darton Longman & Todd, 1994.

John Stevens, *Lust For Enlightenment: Buddhism*, London: Shambhala, 1990.

Elizabeth Stuart, *Chosen: Gay Catholic Priests Tell Their Stories*, London: Geoffrey Chapman, 1993.

Elizabeth Stuart, *Just Good Friends: Towards a Lesbian and Gay Theology of Relationships*, London: Mowbray, 1995.

Elizabeth Stuart, Alison Webster and Gerard Loughlin (eds), *Theology and Sexuality*, No. 1 (September 1994) – No. 15

(September 2001), Sheffield: Sheffield Academic Press, 1994–2001.

Adrian Thatcher, *Liberating Sex: A Christian Sexual Theology,* London: SPCK, 1993.

Thomas Aquinas, *Summa Contra Gentiles*, Chicago: Notre Dame Press, 1975.

Paul Tillich, *The Boundaries of Our Being: A Collection of His Sermons with His Autobiographical Sketch*, London: Fontana, 1973.

Joan Timmerman, *Sexuality and Spiritual Growth*, New York: Crossroad, 1992.

Jean Vanier, *Man and Woman He Made Them*, London: Darton, Longman & Todd, 1985.

Jean Vanier, *The Broken Body*, London: Darton, Longman & Todd, 1988.

William Vanstone, *Love's Endeavour, Love's Expense*, London: Darton, Longman & Todd, 1977.

William Vanstone, *The Stature of Waiting*, London: Darton, Longman & Todd, 1982.

Gordon Wakefield (ed.), *A Dictionary of Christian Spirituality*, London: SCM Press, 1983.

The Way, 'Fragmentation', Vol. 28, No. 4 (October 1988), London: The Way, 1988.

The Way, 'Postmodernism', Vol. 36, No. 3 (July 1996), London: The Way, 1996.

The Way Supplement 86, 'The Spirituality of Children' (Summer 1996), London: The Way, 1996.

James Woodward, *Encountering Illness*, London: SCM Press, 1995.

Therapy and sexual practice

Robert Akeret, *The Man who Loved a Polar Bear and Other Psychotherapists' Tales*, London: Penguin, 1997.

Roger Appignanesi and Oscar Zarate, *Freud for Beginners*, Cambridge: Icon, 1992.

Guy Baldwin, *Ties that Bind*, Los Angeles: Daedalus Publishing Company, 1993.

Joseph Campbell, *The Power of Myth*, New York: Doubleday, 1988.

Mantak Chia and Douglas Abrams Arava, *The Multi Orgasmic Man*, London: Thorsons, 1996.

Nancy Chodorow, *Feminism and Psychoanalytic Theory*, New Haven, CT: Yale University Press, 1989.

Martin Cole and Windy Dryden, *Sex: Why It Goes Wrong and What You Can Do about It*, London: Optima, 1993.

Ram Dass, *Still Here: Embracing Aging, Changing and Dying*, New York: The Berkley Publishing Group, 2001.

Anne Dickson, *The Mirror Within: A New Look at Sexuality*, London: Quartet Books, 1985.

Kat Duff, *The Alchemy of Illness*, London: Virago, 1994.

Sigmund Freud, *Case Histories II*, Penguin Freud Library, Vol. 9, London: Penguin Books, 1991.

Sigmund Freud, *On Sexuality*, Penguin Freud Library, Vol. 7, London: Penguin Books, 1991.

Lasse Hessel, *Windows on Love: The Ultimate Guide to Sexual Fulfilment*, Bathurst: Crawford House, 1992.

John Irwin, Harvey Jackins and Charlie Kreiner, *The Liberation of Men*, Seattle: Rational Island Publishers, 1992.

Harvey Jackins, *A Rational Theory of Sexuality*, Seattle: Rational Island Publishers, 1977.

C. G. Jung, *Memories, Dreams, Reflections*, London: Fontana, 1985.

C. G. Jung (ed.), *Man and His Symbols*, London: Arkana, 1990.

Sarah Litvinoff, *The Relate Guide to Sex in Loving Relationships*, London: Vermilion, 1992.

Patricia Love and Jo Robinson, *Hot Monogamy*, London: Judy Piatkus, 1994.

Margo Maine, *Father Hunger*, London: Simon & Schuster, 1993.

Christiane Olivier, *Jocasta's Children: The Imprint of the Mother*, London: Routledge, 1989.

Alex Pirani, *The Absent Father: Crisis and Creativity*, London: Arkana, 1989.

Anthony Stevens, *Private Myths: Dreams and Dreaming*, London: Penguin, 1995.

Anthony Storr, *Jung*, London: Fontana, 1973.

Ann Ulanov, *The Feminine in Jungian Psychology and in Christian Theology*, Evanston: Northwest University Press, 1971.

Linda Valins, *When a Woman's Body Says No to Sex*, London: Penguin, 1992.

Roy Willis (ed.), *World Mythology*, London: Judy Piatkus, 1997.

Marion Woodman, *The Pregnant Virgin: A Process of Psychological Transformation*, Toronto: Inner City Books, 1985.

Sex surveys

Nancy Friday, *Women on Top: How Real Life Has Changed Women's Sexual Fantasies*, New York: Pocket Books, 1991.

Jonathon Green, *It: Sex Since the Sixties*, London: Martin Secker & Warburg, 1993.

Shere Hite, *The Hite Report on Female Sexuality*, London: Pandora Press, 1989.

Shere Hite, *The Hite Report on Male Sexuality*, London: Macdonald & Co., 1981.

Shere Hite, *The Hite Report on the Family: Growing Up under Patriarchy*, London: Bloomsbury Publishing, 1994.

Shere Hite, *Women as Revolutionary Agents of Change: The Hite Reports 1972–1993*, London: Bloomsbury Publishing, 1993.

Samuel Janus and Cynthia Janus, *The Janus Report on Sexual Behaviour*, New York: John Wiley & Sons, 1993.

Alfred Kinsey, *Sexual Behavior in the Human Male*, Philadelphia: Saunders, 1948.

Susan Quilliam, *Women On Sex*, London: Smith Gryphon, 1994.

Liz Stanley, *Sex Surveyed 1949–1994*, London: Taylor & Francis, 1995.

Kate Wellings, Julia Field, Anne Johnson and Jane Wadsworth, *Sexual Behaviour in Britain*, London: Penguin Books, 1994.

Feminism and the men's movement

Sandra Bem, *The Lenses of Gender: Transforming the Debate on Sexual Inequality*, London: Yale University Press, 1993.

Denise Lardner Carmody, *Responses to 101 Questions about Feminism*, London: Geoffrey Chapman, 1994.

Sally Cline, *Women Celibacy and Passion*, London: Optima, 1994.

Wendy Dennis, *Hot and Bothered: Men and Women, Sex and Love in the 1990's*, London: Grafton, 1992.

Andrea Dworkin, *Intercourse*, London: Arrow Books, 1987.

Eve Ensler, *The Vagina Monologues*, New York: Villard, 2001.

Clarissa Pinkola Estes, *Women Who Run with the Wolves*, London: Rider Books, 1992.

Warren Farrell, *The Myth of Male Power: Why Men Are the Disposable Sex*, London: Simon & Schuster, 1993.

Maureen Freely, *What about Us? An Open Letter to the Mothers Feminism Forgot*, London: Bloomsbury, 1996.

Lorraine Gamman and Merja Makinen, *Female Fetishism: A New Look*, London: Lawrence & Wishart, 1994.

Germaine Greer, *The Female Eunuch*, London: Flamingo, 1970.

Kay Leigh Hagan, *Women Respond to the Men's Movement*, London: Pandora, 1992.

Sam Keen, *Fire in the Belly: On Being a Man*, New York: Bantam, 1991.

Terry Lovell (ed.), *British Feminist Thought: A Reader*, Oxford: Blackwell, 1990.

Neil Lyndon, *No More Sex War: The Failures of Feminism*, London: Sinclair-Stevenson, 1992.

Angela Neustatter, *Hyenas in Petticoats: A Look at Twenty Years of Feminism*, London: Penguin Books, 1990.

Ann Oakley and Juliet Mitchell, *Who's Afraid of Feminism: Seeing through the Backlash*, London: Penguin Books, 1998.

Camille Paglia, *Vamps and Tramps*, London: Penguin Books, 1995.

Janet Radcliffe Richards, *The Sceptical Feminist: A Philosophical Enquiry*, Harmondsworth: Pelican Books, 1982.

Keith Thompson (ed.), *Views from the Male World*, London: The Aquarian Press, 1992.

Ethna Viney, *Dancing to Different Tunes: Sexuality and Its Misconceptions*, Belfast: The Blackstaff Press, 1996.

Alison Webster, *Found Wanting: Women, Christianity and Sexuality*, London: Cassell, 1995.

Sue Wilkerson and Celia Kitzinger, *Heterosexuality: A Feminism and Psychology Reader*, London: Sage, 1993.

Sex and society

Edward Anthony, *Thy Rod and Staff*, London: Abacus, 1996.

John Boswell, *The Marriage of Likeness: Same-Sex Unions in Pre-Modern Europe*, London: Harper Collins, 1995.

Sheron Boyle, *Working Girls and Their Men: A Candid Investigation of Prostitution in Britain*, London: Smith Gryphon, 1994.

Louise Brown, *Sex Slaves: The Trafficking of Women in Asia*, London: Virago Press, 2000.

Lynn Chancer, *Sadomasochism in Everyday Life: The Dynamics of Power and Powerlessness*, New Brunswick: Rutgers University Press, 1992.

Christopher Clulow (ed.), *Women, Men and Marriage: Talks from the Tavistock Marital Studies Institute*, London: Sheldon Press, 1995.

Richard Davenport-Hynes, *Sex, Death and Punishment*, London: Fontana, 1991.

Michel Foucault, *The History of Sexuality: An Introduction*, Harmondsworth: Peregrine, 1984.

Julian Hafner, *The End of Marriage: Why Monogamy Isn't Working*, London: Arrow, 1994.

Lesley Hall, *Sex, Gender and Social Change in Britain Since 1880*, London: Macmillan Press, 2000.

Victoria Harwood, David Oswell, Kay Parkinson and Anna Ward (eds), *Pleasure Principles: Politics, Sexuality and Ethics*, London: Lawrence and Wishart, 1993.

Catherine Itzin (ed.), *Pornography: Women Violence and Civil Liberties: A Radical New View*, Oxford: Oxford University Press, 1992.

Aileen McColgan, *Taking the Date Out of Rape*, London: Pandora, 1996.

John Randall, *Childhood and Sexuality: A Radical Christian Approach*, Pittsburgh: Dorrance, 1992.

Julian Robinson, *The Quest for Human Beauty: An Illustrated History*, London: W. W. Norton, 1998.

Valerie Steele, *Fetish, Fashion, Sex and Power*, Oxford: Oxford University Press, 1996.

Bill Thompson, *Sadomasochism*, London: Cassell, 1994.

Tony Thorne, *Dictionary of Popular Culture: Fads Fashions and Cults*, London: Bloomsbury, 1994.

Neilson Waithe, *Caribbean Sexuality*, Bethlehem USA: The Moravian Church in America, 1993.

Paul Willis, *Common Culture*, Milton Keynes: Open University Press, 1990.

Sex and biology

Richard Dawkins, *The Selfish Gene*, Oxford: Oxford Paperbacks, 1989.

Steve Jones, *In the Blood: God, Genes and Destiny*, London: HarperCollins, 1996.

Lynn Margulis and Dorion Sagan, *Mystery Dance: On the Evolution of Human Sexuality*, London: Simon & Schuster, 1991.

Richard Michod, *Eros and Evolution: A Natural Evolution of Sex*, Wokingham: Helix, 1995.

Desmond Morris, *The Naked Ape*, London: Vintage, 1994.

Desmond Morris, *The Human Sexes: A Natural History of Man and Woman*, London: Network, 1997.

Matt Ridley, *The Red Queen: Sex and the Evolution of Human Nature*, London: Penguin, 1994.

Steven Rose, *Biology, Freedom, Determinism*, London: Penguin, 1997.

Biography and autobiography

John Bayley, *Iris: A Memoir of Iris Murdoch*, London: Abacus, 1999.

Jung Chang, *Wild Swans:Three Daughters of China*, London: Flamingo, 1993.

Ivy George and Margaret Masson, *An Uncommon Correspondence: An East West Conversation on Friendship, Intimacy and Love*, New York: Paulist Press, 1998.

Tony Hawkes, *Round Ireland with a Fridge*, London: Ebury Press, 1998.

Shere Hite, *The Hite Report on Shere Hite: The Voice of a Child in Exile*, London: Arcadia Books, 2000.

Roger Housden and Chloe Goodchild (eds), *We Two*, London: The Aquarian Press, 1992.

The Off Pink Collective, *Bisexual Lives*, London: Off Pink Publishing, 1988.

Sue O'Sullivan and Kate Thomson, *Positively Women: Living with Aids*, 2nd edn, London: Pandora, 1996.

Rachel Silver, *The Girl in the Scarlet Heels: Women in the Sex Business Speak Out*, London: Arrow, 1993.

Rachael Silver, *Where Their Feet Dance: Englishwomen's Sexual Fantasies*, London: Century, 1994.

Andrew Sullivan, *Love Undetectable: Reflections on Friendship, Sex and Survival*, London: Vintage, 1999.
Andrew Sullivan, *Virtually Normal*, London: Picador, 1996.

Erotica

Richard Burton and F. F. Arbuthnot (trs), *The Kama Sutra of Vatsyayana*, London: Mandala, 1992.
Fetish Times, Issue 8, London: Mang Publishing, undated.
Jean-Luc Hennig, *The Rear View: A Brief and Elegant History of Bottoms through the Ages*, London: Souvenir Press, 1996.
John Preston, *Flesh and the Word: An Anthology of Erotic Writing*, London: Plume, 1992.
Margaret Reynolds (ed.), *The Penguin Book of Lesbian Short Stories*, London: Penguin, 1994.
Errol Selkirk, *Erotica for Beginners*, New York: Writers and Readers, 1991.
Skin Two, Issue 18, London: Tim Woodward, 1995.

Overviews

James Doyle and Michele Paludi, *Sex and Gender: The Human Experience*, Dubuque: WCB Brown & Benchmark, 1995.
Kurt Haas and Adelaide Haas, *Understanding Sexuality*, 3rd edn, St Louis: Mosby, 1993.
William Masters, Virginia Johnson and Robert Kolodny, *Heterosexuality*, London: Thorsons, 1994.
Jeffrey Weeks, *Sexuality and Its Discontents: Meanings, Myths and Modern Sexualities*, London: Routlege & Kegan Paul, 1985.

Poetry

T. S. Eliot, *Murder in the Cathedral*, London: Faber & Faber, 1968.

T. S. Eliot, *The Complete Poems and Plays*, London: Faber & Faber, 1969.

The English Hymnal, Oxford: Oxford University Press, 1988.

Ian Hamilton (ed.), *Gerard Manley Hopkins: Selected Poems*, London: Bloomsbury, 1992.

Rainer Maria Rilke, *Letters to a Young Poet*, London: Norton, 1993.

Marilyn Sewell (ed.), *Cries of the Spirit: A Celebration of Women's Spirituality*, Boston: Beacon Press, 1991.

Michael O'Siadhail, *Hail! Madam Jazz*, Newcastle upon Tyne: Bloodaxe, 1992.

All quotations taken from *The Jerusalem Bible*, Popular Edition, London: Darton, Longman & Todd, 1974.

Index